The complete student guide to college beyond the USA

STUDY MAP ABROAD

Wendy Williamson

Printed in the United States of America

International Standard Book Number:

Agapy Publishing
www.agapy.com

–

CONTENTS

INTRODUCTION

One's destination is never a place,
but a new way of seeing things.
— Henry Miller

There's no bones about it; you have to go away so that you can look back and see clearly. You have to leave if you want to learn new things and grow. I went to elementary, middle, and high school in a Midwestern Indiana town. Then I went to Indiana University for college. None of my close relatives had ever left the United States. Why would they? In the last century, people from all over the world had fled their countries to come here, to the land of the free and the brave, to the best nation in the world.

I grew up thinking that my country, the United States of America, had the best of everything. We had the best houses, schools, health care, people, and government. We had the strongest military. We had the most gold. Everyone in the world used our language and currency. We had the best technology, and the list goes on. I felt fortunate to be born in America, and not among all the starving children in Africa. My country was the most powerful, altruistic, generous nation on earth, and was so proud to be American.

This is American exceptionalism, and it comes from propaganda. With international travel and age, I don't believe those things anymore. There are good things about my country, and there are bad things about my country, and I can see it now from the inside and from the outside. I've lived in Cameroon, Ecuador, and Italy, and I see good things and bad things about those countries also. People are different but they are the same. Their cultures are toxic in some ways have healthy in others.

Native American culture was the first one that ever fascinated me. I think it was their close connection to nature, how it guided their ancestors in every aspect of living. I collected Indian artifacts and learned everything I could about them. As a 10-year-old tomboy, I used to run around with a bandana on my head and a feather tucked underneath. I remember the empowering feeling I used to get from beating my bare chest and doing Indian calls outside. I wanted to be an Indian, and regretted being White.

The only thing that really fascinated me about history was the age of exploration and discovery. From a young age, I knew that I was an explorer, but one who would befriend and learn from other people, not conquer them. Until I finished college, the farthest I had ever ventured was Wyoming. I was curious about the rest of the world, but I had to get real and think about how to make my money. My plan was to major in business and become a stockbroker, but I met an obstacle with finite mathematics.

Afraid of failing, I dropped the course, which was a prerequisite for the business school, and had to find another path. My roommate was doing telecommunications, and it sounded fun, so I changed my major to hers. We studied American culture in the media, various genres, and television shows, and the subject captivated me. I don't know what motivated me to join the Peace Corps, but the world mission's organization that I was trying to join turned me down because I didn't have any international experience.

It was somewhere between my cross-cultural communications courses, my required cultural studies courses, my roommate going to Italy, my French language and culture class, my decision to declare an individualized major in communication and culture, and overhearing a conversation in the elevator about the Peace Corps. I remember later seeing a flyer about it. One thing led to another, and I applied. The application process was rigorous, but I got in and placed. Right after college, I left for Africa.

I spent four years in the Peace Corps, first in Cameroon and then in Ecuador. I married a native Ecuadorian who didn't speak English and brought him back with me to the U.S. From there, I pursued a master's degree in higher education administration and started working the field of study abroad. First an advisor and then a director, I built a study-abroad office. In 2014, I was offered a consulting opportunity and moved my family to Italy for two years. To this day, nothing is more exciting to me than exploration. To discover the world's places and people is to discover ourselves.

This book is my way of sharing what I know about international education. It covers the options you have (gap year, study abroad, college abroad, intern abroad, and volunteer abroad), the pros and cons of each, the ins and outs, and step-by-steps. You'll get a clue about the things you should contemplate before you go, while you're away, and when you return. There's lots of useful information that college advisors won't tell you and amateurs don't know. It will help you through processes and logistics, and give you a solid foundation for a positive and successful experience.

So let's get on with it...

STUDY ABROAD MAP

YOU NEED TO KNOW...

1. In the future, a college degree will not be sufficient

The world is a book, and those who do not travel read only a page. — St. Augustine

I'd like to give you a picture of what has happened in the United States over the past 30 years, so that you can understand and think about what might happen in the next 30 years when you'll be employed and maybe raising a family. Since college is a crossroads for your future, this information is invaluable and can change the course of your life. You will not learn this in school, and you will not read this in another study-abroad book. So get a cup of coffee or tea and make yourself comfortable.

In 1989, when I started college at Indiana University Bloomington, my in-state tuition was $2,175. Today, in-state tuition at IU is $10,948. Over the past 30 years, the price has increased a whopping 403 percent. The national debt went from 2.857 trillion to almost 23 trillion today, an even bigger increase of 705 percent. The average points of the Dow went from 2510 to 27398, a humongous 991% increase.

Most people would say this is normal; everything always goes up. But why? When you throw something up, it comes back down, so why should economics be any different? While I didn't major in business, I know that the economic model of supply and demand is relevant. A greater supply of bachelor's degrees has diminished their economic value, and the benefit-cost ratio of a college education has been shrinking, at least in the United States.

If you want to go to college, let's say Indiana University, it's going to cost you at least 403% more than it cost me. You will be borrowing and spending a lot more money to finance a future career that probably won't earn the economic equivalent of what your predecessors earned with their college degrees. Average student loan debt in the United States today is over $1.5 trillion. That's a really big number. If you were to start counting to one trillion in seconds, it would take you 32,000 years!

Going to college has evolved into a rite of passage, but does it really make sense to spend so much money that you don't have and then spend all your time for a long period paying it back? If you can't find a job, you won't get a refund for what feels like an impractical degree. No false advertising claims will be entertained by administrators or faculty. And you'll have to pay back your loans or the banks will be coming after you.

Between artificial intelligence and the government's unlimited borrowing, the unemployment rate will not stay low. The more dollars that government borrows and prints, the less value they will have in the future. The U.S. dollar is strong against other currencies only because the entire world holds it now as the reserve currency. Note my use of the word "now," meaning it's not going to last. The United States didn't earn reserve currency status because we were the good guys and every other country wanted to follow us. The U.S. made an agreement with the rest of the world.

During World War I (1914-18) and II (1939-45), Europe paid the U.S. in gold for guns, tanks, consumer goods, and grains. By the end of World War II, the U.S. had two-thirds of the world's central bank gold and Europe had no gold but lots of dollars that the U.S. had loaned it to buy goods. This made America rich and the other countries poor. Left alone, it would have resulted in a worldwide financial collapse, but representatives from around world met in Bretton Woods, New Hampshire, to find a solution. There, they decided that every currency would be backed by the U.S. dollar and the U.S. dollar would be backed by gold at $35/ounce. Voila, that's why the dollar is the world reserve currency.

In 1944, the dollar literally became as good as gold, because it was backed by gold, and exchange rates were fixed, giving stability to all the world's currencies. The dollar was an IOU (I owe you) for gold and printed on it were the words, "In gold coin payable to the bearer on demand." What that meant was you could walk into any bank and trade $35 for a one ounce gold coin. The United States of America became the world's bank and international trade boomed.

Americans grew rich, powerful, and happy over a short period of time. In Johnson's "Great Society," the U.S. started printing way too many dollars in proportion to its gold backing. Americans forgot that the dollar was an IOU, but when French President Charles de Gaulle caught on to what the U.S. was doing (devaluing the dollar against gold), he spoke publicly about his concerns. It didn't take long until France started sending its IOU dollars back to the U.S. to redeem for gold, which was *real* money. Other countries followed suit, and from 1959 to 1971, the U.S. lost 50% of its gold reserves in return for the dollars other countries were exchanging.

Knowing the U.S. had printed twelve times more dollars than they had gold (oops!), Nixon halted the convertibility of dollars to gold on August 15, 1971. If he hadn't done this, the U.S. would have lost all its gold, and once again, there would have been a monetary system collapse. Do you see what happened? All the world's currencies, once backed by the dollar-equals-gold equation, instantly became fiat, backed by nothing but the full *faith* and *credit* of the U.S. government. I'm not sure what they meant by "credit" but what it ended up being was debt. Your money is backed by debt.

Since that time, our national debt has continued to grow tremendously, and if you understand where that puts the U.S dollar today and where it puts the U.S. economy in the future, then you can see that I'm not on a tangent. Bear with me, this does relate to your college education and your future career. The U.S. is on a borrowing binge, and it's using the world, while it can, to finance everything it thinks it wants and needs in the present. The government is in deep debt, American workers are in deep debt, students like you are in deep debt…where does it end? And what is debt anyway?

Your debt is someone else's investment, and your investment is likely someone else's debt. Someone else lets you borrow his or her money in exchange for an interest rate, and maybe you lend your money to someone else in exchange for the same thing. Since interest rates are so low, there's a lot of money in the stock market, and the companies behind those stocks take out loans to buy back their own stocks, which keeps the prices high and attractive to investors. The gist? It's all a big shit show that will have a very bad ending.

What I have learned from my travels is the United States is not the good guy against a bunch of bad guys in the world. If you get out of the country you can see your American exceptionalism, and you'll begin to understand the truth. The United States is not the big daddy taking care of everyone in the world; it's an empire protecting its own interests, which now is to keep its biggest and most important export in trade. What is that export? Of course, it's the U.S. dollar. If other countries ditch the dollar, all that paper comes home, and that economic model of supply and demand will show.

Lieutenant-General Sir John Bagot Glubb was a British soldier, historian, and author. He studied eleven empires from the Assyrians in 859 B.C. to the British in 1950 A.D. [1] Each empire lasted between 207 to 267 years, and he

---

[1] Sir John Glub. The Fate of Empires and Search for Survival. Accessed on October 22, 2019. http://people.uncw.edu/kozloffm/glubb.pdf

figured out that each followed a remarkably similar pattern from beginning to end, which he articulated in the seven stages listed below:

1. The Age of Pioneers (Outburst)
2. The Age of Conquests
3. The Age of Commerce
4. The Age of Affluence
5. The Age of Intellect
6. The Age of Decadence
7. The Age of Decline & Collapse

It sent chills down my spine when I first read about the seven stages of empire and tagged them through U.S. history. While the settlers arrived in the 1600s, pioneer life developed in two great migrations between 1760 and 1850. From the beginning of America's pioneer age until now, 259 years have passed. Only one of the eleven empires that Glubb studied lasted longer than the United States, and that was the Mameluke Empire (1250-1517).

Decadence, the last stage of empire, is marked by defensiveness, pessimism, materialism, frivolity, an influx of foreigners, the Welfare State, and a weakening of religion. It is the result of too long a period of wealth and power, selfishness, love of money, and loss of a sense of duty. The U.S. became an empire by lending to the world, and it will collapse because it borrowed too much from the world.

When people realize that they've built their lives on sinking green paper (fool's gold), and the U.S. dollar falls from its seat in the sky, they'll remember the motto "In God we Trust," and they'll remember when gold was real money. In the meantime, you've got to figure out your future and how to maximize it through college. There's the benefit-cost ratio, but there's also the value of what you'll gain from the experience. What are you going to learn? How is that going to help you in the future economy? And where will you be able to find work, if not in the United States?

More than being educated, you will have to be smart in the future job market. With the global nature of our workforce, intercultural knowledge and skills will be imperative. A 2014 survey of U.S. business needs for employees with international expertise found that almost 40% of companies surveyed missed global business opportunities because they lacked internationally competent personnel.[2] Missing business opportunities will not be an option when free money printing comes to an end.

I worked in the field of education abroad for a long time, and I know there is a widespread assumption among hiring agents that study abroad is a vacation where college students party hard. This can certainly be true, and I've seen plenty of it. Just as there are students going to college without any clue about what they want to do with their lives, there are students studying abroad with the same cluelessness. That said, if studying abroad is an option for you, be mindful about choosing the right experience and maximizing it. Critical thinking and analysis, as well as creativity and flexibility, are the best skills you can develop in college and the workforce.

Recently, from 2015/16 to 2016/17, the number of U.S. college students studying abroad increased 2.3% to a total of 332,727.[3] According to the National Center for Education Statistics, 19.76 million students attended colleges and universities in the Fall of 2017. Do the math and study abroad is about 3.4 percent. While this number is making administrators happy, a whopping 64.6% of student participation was through short-term programs

---

[2] 2014 U.S. Business Needs for Employees with International Expertise (Executive Summary). Accessed on October 6, 2019. https://www.wm.edu/offices/revescenter/globalengagement/internationalization/papers%20and%20presentations/davidsonkediaexec.pdf

[3] 2018 Open Doors Report. An annual release by the Institute of International Education. Accessed on October 6, 2019. https://www.iie.org/Research-and-Insights/Open-Doors

(summer or less than eight weeks), many of which are highly structured and led by one or more professors. The top location was the United Kingdom (English speaking), and the second most popular was Italy. While Italy is a great country, students don't learn much about Italians or their culture.

If my bias isn't already apparent, I think it's always more beneficial to find an experience that allows you time and ability to immerse in the culture. People with valuable international experience are more creative and better problem solvers; they are more likely to start new businesses, create products, and be promoted.[4] That said, a short-term study abroad program is certainly better than nothing, but there are plenty of superior options.

Picking a college or an international program is like investing in stocks or real estate. Some stocks will take you to the moon, and others will flop miserably. Some real estate will profit bigly and some will cost you dearly. Just because you buy a stock or a piece of real estate or go to college doesn't mean that you'll succeed in life. Think carefully about the future and how your choices now will benefit you later. The best investment you will ever make is your own education.

_____

[4] Harvard Business Review, *Be a Better Manager: Live Abroad* (September, 2010).

2. How to choose the right college if you want to study abroad

The early bird catcheth the worm. — John Ray

If you're planning to study abroad, and you're still in high school, don't skip this section. Use it as a guide to choose a college that will fit your study-abroad dreams.

LEVEL OF SUPPORT
___Is there a study abroad office or officer?
___If so, what is the advisor to student ratio?
___How many students study abroad? And what percentage?
___Is there a good website with information? Is the application online?
___Are the policies, processes, and procedures fair and easy to grasp?
___Do students have positive experiences?

PROGRAM OPTIONS
___Does the college offer any programs that fit you?
___Are there different program types, lengths, and credit?
___If the college doesn't offer a program that fits you, are you allowed to join a external program that you find on your own? If so, how difficult is the process and how likely will the program be approved?
___Will you get valuable credit that is part of your study plan?

ACADEMIC CREDIT
___Will you be enrolled while away? If not, then you will lose all institutional benefits and may have to reapply for admission when you return.
___Are courses pass-fail or graded? Will they average into your GPA or not? Will course titles, grades, and credits appear individually on your transcript or will there be a notation of total transfer credit on your transcript?
___Are study abroad courses linked to your academic requirements? In other words, can you fulfill major, minor, and general education credit or will you get only electives?
___Will your university accept a transcript from any higher education insti-

tution that is recognized by its Ministry of Education or must your courses go through another USA-accredited university for a hefty fee?

FINANCIAL AID
___What financial aid (federal, state, private) can you use for study abroad, and in which study abroad programs can you use it?

___Will the kind of credit you receive affect your financial aid package? Transfer credit may reduce your usable financial aid.

___What are the stipulations for receiving financial aid? For example, some institutions will not give aid to students if they are enrolled in less than six credits.

___Are you enrolled while away? Home institution enrollment is essential for you to receive institutional benefits, financial aid, and scholarships.

___Does the institution offer any scholarships or perks to study abroad?

ACTUAL COSTS
___What are you paying for when you study abroad? It is a good idea to compare costs of similar programs offered through different colleges and universities.

___Where and how do you pay? Sometimes you pay your university and sometimes you pay the provider and host abroad.

___What are the refund policies when you sign on? What is included and not included in the fees? Are any costs hidden? (i.e. transcript processing)

A FEW SCENARIOS TO PONDER

Seemseasy College offers good support. Eight percent of their students study abroad through a limited number of approved program options. Their students are not allowed to participate in other programs, outside of the college. The right program at the right time fulfills curricular requirements and keeps students on track. They can use all of their financial aid and may apply for additional grants and scholarships. It costs $25,000 per semester, all-inclusive.

NoBudget University offers some support, but nothing like Seemseasy College. Only five percent of their students study abroad. There are many more options than Seemseasy College, and students are allowed to participate in other programs through a petition process. The right program at the right time fulfills curricular requirements and keeps students on track. They can use all their financial aid and may apply for additional grants and scholarships. Programs are not all-inclusive like Seemseasy College, but estimated total cost ranges from $1,500 to $12,000 per semester.

OnYourOwn University doesn't provide much support; there is only one faculty member who advises part-time. There is no study abroad office, no website, and no structured programming. The University requires that students withdraw while studying abroad. Students receive transfer credit if they have a transcript sent to the university. They cannot use financial aid unless they move it to another qualified provider. Students find programs on their own and take care of all arrangements, including payment.

Proprietary College has a study abroad office and an adequate support staff. They have fifteen program options, and students can obtain permission to participate in a non-Proprietary program. They award university credit for their programs and transfer credit for others, but they only allow you to use financial aid for *their* programs. The cost varies per program but ranges from $8,000 to $18,000 for a semester abroad.

3. Gap year can be very beneficial if you plan carefully

Don't ask what the world needs. Ask what makes you come alive, because what the world truly needs is people who have come alive. — Howard Thurman

Gap year is an annual break from traditional schooling, taken between high school and college. Students who take gap years may or may not know what they want to study during college, and this time can help them figure it out. According to the American Gap Year Association, many Ivy League universities appreciate the idea of gap year and encourage prospective students to take one. Others have built a similar experience into their curriculum, such as Harvard, Princeton, UNC, Duke, and Tufts. Visit <u>americangap.org/fav-colleges.php</u> for more information.

By no means is gap year for everyone. If you don't know yet what you want to study, then gap year could help you decide. It depends on how you integrate the experience with your interests. If you're exploring a potential career, then taking a gap year that exposes you to the real world of that career can be a very important step. Whether it's marine biology and you volunteer on a research vessel, or business and you focus on learning another language, or education and you assistant-teach in Tanzania. Any of these will help. A wise man once said, if you love what you do, you'll never have to work, so discovering what you love is time well invested.

There is a ton of information on the Internet and lots of programs, many of which are commercial. When I went to college, there was no Internet or email or cellulars, so I didn't know that gap year was even an option. Since my family never traveled, it didn't occur to me that I could, until I learned about it during college. If you know what you want to study, you might want to just get on with it, but if you're unsure, then it's not a bad idea to do something else. You can work, volunteer, or go travel around Europe and meet other people your age. Maybe you'll find that you don't want to go to college in the U.S. but in one of the countries you landed.

4. Consider going to college in another country

Towering genius disdains a beaten path. It seeks regions hitherto unexplored.
— Abraham Lincoln

While study abroad consists of a break, summer, quarter, semester, or academic year, it's possible to spend even more time away by choosing a joint or dual degree option. A single diploma that is awarded by two or more institutions is a *joint degree.* Two separate diplomas, one from each institution, is a *dual degree.* In either case, there will be a significant amount of time spent at both universities, one of which may be in the United States. You can search the Internet for international joint-degree programs or international dual-degree programs that are sponsored by U.S. colleges and universities.

There are also compelling reasons to do your undergraduate and/or graduate degree abroad. You can apply and attend a college or university in another country, and you don't need a foreign language to do so. Personally, I would not have been ready after high school to move to another country, but I would have considered it for a graduate degree. But if you're adventurous and enjoy being independent, there's no reason why *you* can't get a college degree abroad. I'm hoping my son will consider a university outside of the states, and I'll help him all that I can with his decision-making process and the logistics of moving to another country.

As a study abroad director, my experience is that most U.S. students need a fair amount of assistance when they go off to college. There are some go-getters, but they're rare. It's not your fault if you don't feel ready to leave your country for many years, and it's not your parent's fault either; it's cultural for the most part. U.S. higher education institutions provide a lot more support and services than European institutions. When we lived in Italy, my son sat in the same chair all day while the teachers rotated classrooms. He was expected to go to high school Monday thru Saturday, and there was a lot more homework too.

Every place will vary, and comes with pros and cons. The most expensive college is in the United Kingdom and United States. The less expensive are in Europe, while Canada, Australia and Asia are in-between. Latin America public vs private varies. If you speak Spanish, and are comfortable taking your classes in Spanish, a Latin American university could be a wonderful opportunity. There are some very good universities in Latin America, including Pontificia Universidad Católica de Chile (PUC), Universidad Veritas in Costa Rica, Pontificia Universidad Católica del Perú (PUCP), Universidad San Francisco de Quito (USFQ), University of Havana, and more.

In Europe, Germany and France are probably the least expensive. Public university is Germany is virtually $0 and France is just a couple hundred dollars. European undergraduate degrees are usually three years instead of four, and there are fewer general education requirements. Europeans decide what to study in high school, and narrow their focus in college. College is rigorous and structured, and there isn't room to explore. If you already know what you want to study, Europe could be a good fit, but it's not well suited for wandering. College campuses tend to be more integrated with city life in Europe too. They may be spread out in many different locations.

Generalizing, I'd say that European students tend to be more mature, educated, and independent than American students. They know more about global affairs, and they're conversant in several different languages. If anything is to blame for America's immaturity, it's the empire. Ever go to the grocery store and see blueberries from Argentina? Ask yourself, if we grow them here in the United States, which we do, why are grocery chains bringing them all the way from Argentina? Do Argentine blueberries taste better than ours? No, it's cheaper even after transportation costs for us to buy outside of our country than it is to buy here. Why? Because the dollar is our number one export.

Right now in history, the Argentines want dollars because their currency, the Argentine peso, fell 52% against the dollar in 2018, while interest rates have gone up a whopping sixty percent in their country! Imagine if the interest rates on your visa, or mortgage, or car loan went up to sixty percent next week. It doesn't take a brain surgeon to figure out what that would do to the economy. International education is learning and understanding how the world works. So if you're interested in being internationally educated, consider why this is happening in a country like Argentina with 101 billion in debt and not in the U.S. with 23 trillion indebted.

The devaluation of the Argentine peso, and the current economic crisis, was caused by a fluctuation of external debt in U.S. dollars. Since the dollar is the reserve currency, the whole world uses it for lending and trade. This means the whole world is affected by what we do with it. When the Feds were tightening, reducing the balance sheet, and raising interest rates, world investors started pulling out cash from Argentina and redeploying it back into the U.S. This caused the dollar to strengthen, and countries with high external financing, like Argentina and Turkey, to get killed. Why? Because their debt, priced in dollars, suddenly got a lot more expensive against their sinking currencies.

My point is our lives are easier and we don't have to work as hard or struggle as much because the whole world has financed America for a very long time. They do this because they hold and use our dollars for oil, trade, and banking. We print; they buy. But that's changing. The biggest two foreign holders of treasury securities[5] are Japan and China. As of July, 2019, Japan held about $1.13 trillion and China held $1.11 trillion. Russia dumped all its treasuries, but total foreign ownership is still at a record high of $6.63 trillion. The Fed is starting to lower rates again to stimulate the economy, but either way there will be consequences. Raising rates will crash the stock market, and lowering them will devalue the dollar.

If you want to learn more about going to college in Europe, get a copy of *College Abroad* by Holly Oberle. She did her undergraduate and graduate degrees in Germany and now she is an Assistant Professor at The American

---

[5] Accessed on October 11, 2019. https://ticdata.treasury.gov/Publish/mfh.txt

University in Cairo. Another book is *College Beyond the States* by Jennifer Viemont, and a website https://beyondthestates.com with free articles and a paid advisory service for students who would like to explore English-taught college in Europe that won't break the bank. I mentioned European institutions, but there are also plenty of American colleges and universities abroad. You can find them by searching for foreign institutions that accept U.S. financial aid. Go to the Federal School Code Search on the FAFSA site: fafsa.ed.gov/FAFSA/app/schoolSearch. Under the *State* field, select "Foreign Country." Currently, there are 420 schools on the list.

5. Your study abroad courses replace academic requirements

Experience, travel…these are an education in themselves. — Euripides

Most U.S. colleges and universities pre-approve study abroad courses for curricular requirements, but you'll need to ask about the rules. Can you get credit for courses taken at international institutes and centers? Are there limits on the number of credits you can earn or restrictions on time you can spend away? Are you allowed to transfer courses taken in all subject areas?

You may also encounter rules at your institution abroad, especially if you direct enroll. Sometimes foreign students are not allowed to take certain courses that have prerequisites or require a full year of study (i.e. nursing). Courses can also be cancelled if there aren't enough students enrolled, in which case having a back-up plan is important.

When it comes to processing credit for study abroad, every university does it differently. Some record grades and factor them into your grade point average. Some record grades but don't factor them into your grade point average. Still others award pass, fail, and/or transfer credit, regardless of the grades you receive abroad.

| Peace in the Middle East | A | 3 credit |
| International Management | B | 3 credit |

or

Transfer...6 credits

LESS COMMON TYPES OF CREDIT

Internship Credit offers students an opportunity to gain important international work experience. Study abroad internships are usually initiated by a student, and arranged in collaboration with an academic department or within the parameters of a study abroad program.

Independent study may be available to self-motivated students for research or other international learning experiences that are conducted outside of the classroom environment. Students may propose an idea to any regular fulltime member of their faculty.

Experiential Credit is for students who have acquired certain competencies, indisputably equivalent to or superior to those that could have been acquired on the home campus. This type of credit should not be overlooked by students who have lived, studied, or worked extensively abroad.

Examination credit may be awarded if, after an international experience, a student passes an exam designed to measure the learning objectives of the study-abroad courses that were taken abroad. This is more common with foreign-language learning.

6. You can do an internship abroad instead of taking courses

The world is your school. — Martin H. Fischer

There are different ways that you can do an internship abroad. The cheapest is to organize something on your own, in cooperation with your study abroad office or one of your professors. Sometimes professors have contacts in organizations or corporations looking for help, but you can also contact an agency that specializes in this. Agencies may offer interview assistance, job placement, housing, visa help, customer support, and language lessons.

To obtain credit for an internship, you will need to have the experience pre-approved by your university. Don't go on your own without pre-approval. You can usually get credit with an official transcript from the agency showing that you completed their internship course, or by working out an independent study course with a professor from your school.

If you're interested in foreign policy or another international career, consider working with a domestic organization that has an international focus or branch. See the websites of big NGOs, the U.S. Department of State, and the Foreign Policy Association for possibilities. The federal, state, and city governments may have internships in their international trade offices.

A great place to start is Michigan State's International Internship Directory: globaledge.msu.edu/international-internships. You can find international internship opportunities offered by two- and four-year colleges and universities, governmental agencies, non-profit groups, private organizations, and corporations.

7. Studying abroad doesn't have to delay graduation

Nothing happens unless first a dream. — Carl Sandburg

If you plan carefully and your courses are pre-approved for curricular re-quirements, then you shouldn't have a problem graduating on time. You can actually speed up your graduation if that's what you want to do. I've seen Spanish majors complete all their language requirements in one or two semesters, and German majors get twenty credits for one semester of study abroad. It depends on the program you choose, the credit evaluation pro-cess, and the norms at your college or university.

Education majors usually have a hard time studying abroad during the aca-demic year because of certification requirements, but they can participate in summer programming or do their student teaching overseas through or-ganizations like Consortium of Overseas Teaching (COST). Your institu-tion would need to be a member of the consortium.

Beware if you study abroad in the term before you are planning to graduate and you need the coursework for graduation. It takes longer for universities to receive international transcripts and process grades. Every year, there are disappointed students who cannot participate in graduation ceremonies because their international transcripts did not arrive in time.

YOU NEED TO KNOW...

8. If you only speak English, you can still study abroad

A man who does not know a foreign language is ignorant of his own.
— Johann Wolfgang von Goethe

You don't need to know a foreign language in order to study abroad. There are more options available if you speak another language, or want to learn another language, but knowing a foreign language before you go is not a requirement and doesn't have to be a part of your international education experience.

Australia, New Zealand, parts of Africa, Canada, Ireland, and the United Kingdom are all English-speaking areas, which provide valuable cultural experiences to students. However, you'll still have to deal with language barriers. Sometimes English language barriers can be more difficult than learning a foreign language.

"A good screw" in British means "a good salary" in American English, not our coarser version. If going to the United Kingdom, check out *The (Very) Best of British: the American's Guide to Speaking British* at effingpot.com, or the British to American Translator at translatebritish.com.

Of course, there are many opportunities to study abroad in non-English speaking countries, too. Italy is the second leading study abroad destination for U.S. college students,[6] but the majority of U.S. students do not speak Italian. You can choose from a list of English-taught courses at foreign universities and institutes. Alternatively, you can study at an American university overseas. Some students do both.

9. It doesn't have to cost a fortune to study abroad

Wealth is the ability to fully experience life. — Henry David Thoreau

---

[6] Based on the most current data from the Institute of International Education's *Open Doors Report* and the U.S. Department of Education's National Center for Education Statistics.

STUDY ABROAD MAP

You can study abroad for less than it costs you now to attend college in the U.S. How is this possible? As an incentive to go, many U.S. universities waive their own tuition so that students can pay the institution abroad. If you choose a country with a low cost of living, you save there too.

LOW COST OF LIVING	HIGH COST OF LIVING
Athens (Greece), Buenos Aires (Argentina), Lisbon (Portugal), Prague (Czech Rep), Quito (Ecuador), San Jose (Costa Rica), Santiago (Chile), Sofia (Bulgaria), Warsaw (Poland)	Amsterdam, Beijing, Copenhagen, Dublin, Geneva, Hong Kong, London, Milan, Madrid, Moscow, Osaka, Oslo, Paris, Rome, Seoul, Singapore, Shanghai, Sydney, St. Petersburg, Tokyo, Vienna, Zurich

While cost of living is important, it is sometimes unavoidable. If you're an English major, London may be the perfect destination. Believe it or not, you can find less expensive programs even in London and live in a cost-effective area. The key is to have a budget and stick to it. Pay attention to details like what's included in the program fee and what's not, and figure out your total estimated cost. Consider tuition, fees, passport, visa, immunizations, insurance, housing, food, utilities, airfare, transportation to and from the airport, local weekly transportation, books, supplies, and excursions.

10. Federal financial aid can be used for study abroad

I know at last what distinguishes man from animals; financial worries. — Romain Rolland

Federal financial aid can be used for study abroad if (a) credit is earned and (b) the home institution approves the academic credit earned toward the student's degree. The law states that students cannot be denied federal aid simply because they are studying abroad.

The only type of federal aid that is difficult to use outside of a FAFSA School is *work-study*, because of reporting requirements. However, it is sometimes possible to convert a work-study award into a Perkins loan. Ask your financial aid officer for more information.

FAFSA is the first step to any type of public aid or assistance: grants (Pell, TEACH, FSEOG, SMART, etc.), Plus and Stafford loans, Perkins loans, public state funding, and many study abroad scholarships. It is based on financial need according to your Estimated Family Contribution (EFC). Visit studentaid.ed.gov after January 1 and complete the FAFSA by June 30, or your state's deadline.

The financial aid office will use your program budget to calculate financial aid for the semester. With most aid, you will need to maintain full-time status in an accredited degree-granting program, and have your study abroad courses pre-approved for credit. More aid is available for *resident credit* than for *transfer credit*, so if you're finding it difficult to use your regular aid, choosing an exchange program may help, since exchange students are usually registered for resident credit.

There are many grants and scholarships earmarked for study abroad. I know several students who received more money than needed for their study abroad experience. One bought a laptop and a camera with his extra funds. Others have used their excess to travel around Europe. The most notorious awards favor nontraditional and non-English-speaking locations.

11. Grants and scholarships are everywhere you look

People who say it cannot be done, should not interrupt those who are doing it.
— George Bernard Shaw

Study abroad scholarships are everywhere. Some are *merit-based* and some are *need-based*. Some are for students with a particular demographic background (gender, race, and ethnicity), while others revolve around a specific destination, program, type, length, or subject. You just have to know where to look for them and how to apply. It's not uncommon for application deadlines to be a year or more in advance, so the earlier you get started, the more likely you will receive an award that can help defray costs.

Most scholarship applications require a personal statement or essay. Look at this as an opportunity to convince the committee that you are one of their best candidates. Submit a unique essay for each application. Focus on your education and how studying in another country will enhance your career goals. Write with enthusiasm, unifying academic achievements, personal beliefs, and key experiences into an attractive theme. Include significant experiences, but not too many.

After you've finished, re-read and re-write your essays, checking for gaps and errors. Take them to your university's writing center and study abroad office for a critique. Eliminate any unnecessary length and redundancy. Be sure that your writing demonstrates desirable traits like flexibility, maturity, adaptability, communication, independence, leadership potential, commitment to a better world, and clear goals for a successful experience.

There are many websites where you can start your search for scholarships, including the University of Minnesota Scholarships Database (the URL changes frequently). You can also check with employers, associations, organizations, churches, clubs, social groups, fraternities and sororities. Here are the most popular scholarships for which students compete:

BENJAMIN A. GILMAN INTERNATIONAL SCHOLARSHIP
iie.org/gilman

This scholarship, sponsored by the U.S. Department of State's Bureau of Educational and Cultural Affairs, is for students with financial need to pursue study abroad, international internships, and service learning opportunities for at least four weeks in one country. Preference is given to students of diverse ethnic backgrounds, students with high financial need, students with disabilities, and first-generation college students enrolled in community colleges, studying in non-traditional locations, and doing career-oriented internships abroad. Applicants must be U.S. citizens and undergraduates in good academic standing and eligible for a Pell Grant. Up to $5000 (Critical Need Language Awards are $8,000). Apply in April and October.

BOREN AWARDS FOR INTERNATIONAL STUDY
borenawards.org

This award, sponsored by the National Security Education Program, is for students to study less commonly taught languages in regions of the world that the United States seeks to know better. This includes Africa, Asia, Central and Eastern Europe, Eurasia, Latin America and the Caribbean, and the Middle East. Applicants must be U.S. citizens and undergraduates working toward a college degree in the United States. Preference is given to those who are planning to study for a full academic year. Undergraduates receive up to $20,000 and graduates receive up to $30,000. The deadline is in late January for the following academic year.

CRITICAL LANGUAGE SCHOLARSHIP PROGRAM
clscholarship.org

This award, sponsored by the U.S. Department of State's Bureau of Educational and Cultural Affairs, offers intensive summer language institutes for 7 to 10 weeks in thirteen critical foreign languages. The institutes cover an academic year of university-level language coursework during a seven- to ten-week program, designed to meet the needs of students from a variety of language levels and backgrounds. Some institutes require two years of prior language study (or equivalent), while others accept students with no prior knowledge of the language. Students may go where people speak Arabic, Azerbaijani, Bangla/Bengali, Chinese, Hindi, Indonesian, Japanese, Korean, Persian, Punjabi, Russian, Turkish, and Urdu languages taught at summer institutes in Azerbaijan, Bangladesh, China, Egypt, India, Indonesia, Japan, Jordan, Korea, Morocco, Oman, Russia, and Turkey. The scholarship covers airfare, tuition, room and board, overseas health benefits, and visa fees. Participants also receive a small stipend to cover incidental expenses and meals not provided by the program. The deadline is in November.

FULBRIGHT U.S. STUDENT SCHOLARSHIPS
us.fulbrightonline.org
This scholarship, sponsored by the U.S. Department of State's Bureau of Educational and Cultural Affairs, was established in 1946 by Congress to increase mutual understanding by the people of the United States and the people of more than 140 other countries. It may be used for studying, teaching, or conducting research abroad. Applicants must be U.S. citizens and graduating seniors (or hold a B.S., B.A., master's degree, or be a doctoral candidate or young professional or artist). Students may study in East Asia, Pacific Region, Europe and Eurasia, Near East, North Africa, South and Central Asia, Sub-Saharan Africa and the Western Hemisphere. The deadline is in October for the following academic year.

FUND FOR EDUCATION ABROAD
fundforeducationabroad.org
FEA is committed to reducing financial restrictions through the provision of grants and scholarships. Candidates are U.S. undergraduates committed to supporting education abroad by working on campus upon return. Students commit a minimum of four weeks, and receive up to $10,000. Visit the website in November for application information and deadlines.

LANGUAGE FLAGSHIP PROGRAM
thelanguageflagship.org
The Language Flagship is a national initiative designed to change the way Americans learn languages. Undergraduate students commit to learning one of ten languages critical to U.S. national security and economic com-

petitiveness. To be eligible, you must be a U.S. citizen and undergraduate with an advanced-low proficiency in one of the following languages: Arabic, Chinese, Hindi, Korean, Persian, Portuguese, Russian, Swahili, Turkish and Urdu. If selected, you attend one of 22 universities and colleges across the United States, combined with overseas study opportunities at one of ten flagship centers. This is a two-year commitment, both domestic and overseas. The program covers tuition, a modest stipend, and support for health insurance and travel costs. The deadline is in January.

ROTARY AMBASSADORIAL SCHOLARSHIP
rotary.org
Funded by the Rotary Foundation for graduate study in a field related to Rotary's objectives (world peace, international understanding, eliminating disease, conquering hunger, or fostering literacy) for an academic year. Applicants must contact their nearest Rotary Club. Students who apply early may receive up to $26,000. It varies by district, but generally, application is one and a half years in advance.

ROTARY FOUNDATION SCHOLARSHIP
rotary.org
Funded by the Rotary Foundation to undergo intensive study of a foreign language and cultural immersion for three to six months. Applicants must contact their nearest Rotary Club to apply, and must have at least one year of training in the language to be studied. There are 15 languages offered in 29 countries The award may vary between $10,000 to $15,000. The deadline varies by district, but generally it's one and a half years in advance.

BRIDGING SCHOLARSHIP (US-JAPAN)
bridgingfoundation.org
Funded by the Association of Teachers of Japanese Bridging Project, this scholarship is for undergraduate students who have been accepted in a program in Japan for a semester or longer. Must be a U.S. citizen or permanent resident, working on an undergraduate degree in the United States. Recipients get $2,500 (semester) or $5,000 (academic year). The deadline is in April for the fall or academic year and October for the spring.

CHINESE GOVERNMENT SCHOLARSHIPS
https://www.chinesescholarshipcouncil.com/scholarships-in-china
This scholarship is for non-Chinese undergraduate and graduate students to enroll in a degree program in China, taught in Chinese.

FREEMAN-ASIA SCHOLARSHIP
iie.org/programs/freeman-asia
This scholarship is funded by the Institute of International Education and is for U.S. citizens with freshmen, sophomore, and junior standing, with demonstrated financial need, who are planning to study in East or Southeast Asia for a summer (eight weeks or longer), semester, or year. For the summer, students receive up to $3000; for a semester, up to $5000; for an academic year up to $7000. The deadline is in March for summer, April for fall or academic year, and October for spring.

GEORGE J. MITCHELL SCHOLARSHIP (US-IRELAND)
us-irelandalliance.org
This scholarship is funded by the USA-Ireland Alliance for an academic year. Scholars must be enrolled in a graduate degree program or certificate program offered in Ireland or Northern Ireland, and must be a U.S. citizen between 18 and 30 years of age with academic excellence, outstanding leadership, and a strong commitment to community and service. The award covers tuition, housing, a $12,000 stipend, and travel. The deadline is in October for the following academic year.

GERMAN ACADEMIC EXCHANGE SERVICE (DAAD) SCHOLARSHIPS
daad.org
These scholarships are available to undergraduate and graduate students with well-defined research, internships, study projects, or summer courses at German universities. Applicants must be planning to study or conduct research in Germany. Awards range from $2,000 to actual expenses.

JAPANESE (MONBUKAGAKUSHO) SCHOLARSHIP
https://www.studyjapan.go.jp/en/toj/toj0302e.html
This scholarship is funded by the Japanese government for research stu-

dents, teacher training students, undergraduate students, Japanese studies, and technology. There is no application form; the host university (in collaboration with the home university) submits nominations on your behalf.

JASSO SHORT-TERM STUDENT EXCHANGE SCHOLARSHIP (JAPAN)
www.jasso.go.jp

This scholarship is funded by the Japan Student Services Organization and is designed to promote friendships. To qualify, you must be participating in a Japanese academic-year exchange program from three months to one year in length. It provides for a stipend of ¥80,000 per month, and a relocation allowance of about ¥150,000 upon arrival. There is no application form, but the host university (in collaboration with the home university) submits nominations at the time you apply to the program.

MARSHALL SCHOLARSHIP (UNITED KINGDOM)
marshallscholarship.org

The British government established this full-ride scholarship to thank the United States for its assistance during World War II. It is for two years of graduate study in the United Kingdom, at any university. This scholarship is competitive, see the website, and you must graduate with a 3.7 GPA or higher. Awards vary according to circumstances, place of residence, and selected university, but tend to be about £20,000 per year on average. Submit the application in mid-September, at least two or more years before obtaining a bachelor's degree.

RHODES SCHOLARSHIP (OXFORD IN THE UNITED KINGDOM)
rhodesscholar.org

Funded by the Rhodes Trust, this full-ride scholarship provides generous stipends for study at Oxford in the United Kingdom for two years with the possibility of renewal. Recipients must be between 18 and 24 years old and complete a bachelor's degree. You should apply by October 1, in the fall of your senior year.

12. Advisors don't tell you everything

The only true wisdom is in knowing you know nothing. — Socrates

Your advisors won't tell you everything. It's not that they're trying to hide things or deceive you; it's just not their place. Ultimately, it is your life and your responsibility to gather good information and use it in the most effective way possible, but here are some things to keep in mind:

1. It isn't uncommon for a private institution to charge full tuition, in excess of $20,000, for an outsourced program that costs under $8,000. Advisors won't tell you this, but you may be able to participate in the same study-abroad program for a lot less money by going through another U.S. institution or direct enrolling on your own. By direct enrolling, you can transfer your academic credit for a huge discount, as long as your host institution is recognized by its Ministry of Education.

2. Advisors can't tell you what program to choose. Their job is to guide you, not to push you. Study abroad offices sponsor a whole portfolio of programs that they promote equally. On the other hand, faculty who are leading programs abroad should and will try to convince you to go. They have to find enough students, or their program will be cancelled.

3. Advisors won't usually tell you if the program might be cancelled due to low enrollment or if you've chosen a program with a sketchy reputation, poor academic standards, or other problems. Not all programs are equal. It's up to you to do the research before you make a decision. I can't tell you how many returning students wish they had done a better job at researching their program.

4. They won't usually tell you about alternatives to studying abroad, like going to college abroad to pursue an undergraduate or graduate degree. If you're interested in this, and you need U.S. federal financial aid, use the School Code Search: https://fafsa.ed.gov/FAFSA/app/schoolSearch.

Under the State field, select "Foreign Country" and search to get a list of all colleges abroad that accept U.S. federal financial aid.

5. Most advisors won't know about which housing option is the best for you. They manage many programs that they have never visited. What they know is based on previous student experiences and email messages back and forth with the host. Again, this is where good research is useful. Housing is an extremely important part of your experience and you don't want to end up in a place that is uncomfortable or problematic.

6. They generally won't tell you if they favor a certain provider over another, or a certain program in the same city as another. Sometimes you have the choice of going to the same city in many different ways (faculty-led, direct-enroll partnership, external provider). You will have to figure out what is best for you and your pocketbook. Not all programs are the same and there are vast differences even in the same city.

PERSONAL CONSIDERATIONS

13. Religion

Where knowledge ends, religion begins. — Benjamin Disraeli

People don't usually talk about religion, especially if it's likely to result in disagreement. Nonetheless, religion may be a factor in your decision to study abroad.

I lived with a fantastic Animistic Muslim family while training with the Peace Corps. We exchanged much dialog about God, and I questioned both their religious views and mine. Overall, it was a positive experience. Their commitment to Allah made me think about my commitment to Jehovah and deepened my own faith as a Christian. It allowed me to see my religion and myself from a different perspective.

Africa, South America, Europe, and the Middle East are often considered a goldmine of religious relics and can be a wonderful place to learn and undertake study and research. Studying religion in its birthplace or early stages of evolution can be an eye-opening experience to say the least.

If you are very religious, and overtly practice your religion, be sure to investigate its acceptance in the country you wish to visit. Some countries don't tolerate the beliefs or practices of certain religions, and it would be best for you to either not go to one of those countries or not exhibit your beliefs while there. The most popular study-abroad destinations are tolerant of different religions and beliefs, although one may dominate the culture.

14. Graduate student

Education is a progressive discovery of our ignorance. — Will Durant

Graduate students usually have two major concerns when it comes to study abroad: (a) fulfilling academic requirements with little flexibility, and (b) financing the experience, since graduate assistantships aren't usually transportable off-campus.

In many cases, graduate students can complete internships, practicum, and electives abroad. They may also travel abroad for teaching and research purposes. If you're researching any human subjects, don't forget that each participant must provide *informed consent*.

For a short-term experience, there are many faculty-led programs looking for students within particular disciples. In Student Affairs, I've seen many over the years: Disability in a Diverse Society (Michigan State), Issues in College Student Development (St. Cloud State), International Perspective on Education and Social Reform (New York University), and Comparing Educational Systems (Clemson University). These can be an excellent way for graduate students to go abroad without a great deal of planning.

For long-term experiences, consider going to graduate school abroad. Holly Oberle, in her book *College Abroad*, discusses how to do this right, drawing on her own personal experiences while pursing two graduate degrees in Germany.

15. Partner or children

Rejoice with your family in the beautiful land of life! —Albert Einstein

If it is your dream to study abroad, don't let anything get in your way. More nontraditional students are going back to college, and more study abroad programs are taking spouses and children into consideration. Children and spouses can benefit from your studying abroad just as much as you can, and it's good for them too. While it takes preparation to make special arrangements, your study-abroad office can help with this process.

I helped a single Mexican-American student take her eight-year old daughter with her to Mexico. Both had a wonderful and unforgettable experience returning to their motherland and learning about their ancestral heritage. Mom took classes at the university, and her daughter attended an American-style elementary school. They particularly enjoyed living with a host family that took care of their everyday needs like cooking and laundry, while they focused on their studies.

The Office of Overseas Schools, in the U.S. Department of State, provides a directory of elementary and secondary schools for dependents of U.S. citizens living and working abroad. Transitionsabroad.com provides resources for families, including books, articles, exchanges, rentals, homestays, and hostels. The Internet is a never-ending wealth of information.

16. Ethnic minority

Almost always, the creative dedicated minority has made the world better.
— Martin Luther King, Jr.

If you are a student of color who plans to study somewhere that is devoid of color, you may have questions. Will you encounter racial bias and prejudice? Will people make unfair judgments based on the color of your skin? How will things be different from what you experienced at home? What things will be the same?

On the contrary, you may be excited if you are going to a part of the world where you will represent a member of the majority for the first time in your life. How will it feel to see your own race everywhere, from the taxi driver all the way up to the president? How will locals perceive you? How will your culture be different from theirs?

To have a successful study abroad experience, it is important to investigate your race in different countries. Whether gawked at or glanced over, you should at least know what to expect and how to respond. A few noteworthy combinations are blacks in Spain, China, and Japan; Koreans in Ecuador; Native Americans in Russia; and whites in Japan.

If you are white, then you may be considered a minority in certain areas of the world. As a result, you may learn what it feels like to represent the minority in a culture, similar to what people of color experience in many parts of the United States. While it doesn't compare to a lifetime of being a minority in any nation, it's a good experience.

I once advised a member of the college football team, who studied abroad in Japan. People gawked and laughed at him, and called him a giant. Some even stopped to take his picture because he looked so strange and different to them. He decided to come home early, halfway through his program. It's easy to forget that people are learning about you just as much as you are about them.

17. Disability or challenge

Courage and strength is not the absence of fear; it's refusing to assume the role of a victim.
— Anne Wafula Strike

There are two federal laws in place to protect the educational rights of individuals with disabilities. The first is *Section 504 of the Rehabilitation Act of 1973*. This law strictly prohibits discrimination on the sole basis of disability in any program or activity receiving federal financial assistance. According to the *Civil Rights Restoration Act of 1987*, if a higher education institution accepts even one U.S. dollar of federal funding anywhere, in any area or department, then this law applies to the entire institution.

The second is Title II of the Americans with Disabilities Act (ADA). This law applies to all government and commercial entities, including study abroad. It prohibits discrimination against individuals with qualified disabilities in all services, programs, and activities, regardless of whether they are public or private.

In light of these laws and our inability to control situations and circumstances in other countries, most universities strive to provide reasonable accommodation, unless it would fundamentally alter the study abroad program. It is however, the responsibility of the student to disclose a disability to the appropriate campus official, early in the process, and be clear about the type of assistance needed.

Mobility International USA (MIUSA), serves as the National Clearinghouse on Disability and Exchange (NCDE). This organization strives to increase study abroad opportunities for people with disabilities and provide student assistance that helps ensure successful international experiences. Visit their website at miusa.org. It is full of information, as well as publications, videos, and programs. Consider one of their books, *Survival Strategies for Going Abroad: Strategies for People with Disabilities*.

Another source of information is Access Abroad at the University of Minnesota: umabroad.umn.edu/professionals/accessabroad. It is a collaborative work among many universities, and is considered a national resource in the field of international education. See their sampling of programs around the world that accommodate students with disabilities, and the section that highlights student experiences.

While there may not be countless options for students with physical disabilities, more universities around the world are becoming accessible. Whatever your needs, it is important to be proactive in your program search. Be open and honest with your advisor and disability services coordinator about the kind of accommodations you need. It is critical to find the right program and support for a successful experience abroad.

18. Nontraditional student

Our greatest glory is not in never falling but in rising every time we fall. — Confucius

If you're a nontraditional student, and you are planning to study abroad, age-diversity can be a good thing. Chances are you'll enjoy this unique opportunity to interact primarily with a new generation of students. You may be able to offer them a positive perspective throughout their studies. On the other hand, you may find yourself doing things that you never thought feasible or possible at your age.

Whether or not to live in the residence halls is up to you, but I've found that older students either prefer to live apartment-style or with a host family. It really depends on your way of life, your goals, and your flexibility. It also depends on the culture. In France, for example, host families usually don't work out as well as they do in Spain or Latin America. Sometimes host families don't work at all for adults who are accustomed to living by themselves and on their own.

If you can make the commitment, the U.S. Peace Corps is an excellent way to live and work in another culture without the typical worries that come with studying abroad. The Peace Corps pays for international and local transportation, language and technical training, healthcare services, and provides an adequate salary to sustain you. In addition, the Peace Corps sets aside a monthly mini-retirement stipend, available after your service. I met many retirees in the Peace Corps who were having the time of their lives.

19. Dietary restrictions

One cannot think well, love well, sleep well, if one has not dined well.
— Virginia Woolf, A Room of One's Own

Students with dietary restrictions need to plan accordingly. If you live with a host family, they should be able to accommodate your needs. If you live on your own, it's a lot easier to decide what to eat and not to eat, but there are also drawbacks and other considerations.

In some countries, it will be challenging to keep a special diet. Vegetarians in Spain don't have many options when eating out, since Spaniards eat a lot of meat. You can't always prepare your own food because it's cultural to dine out. I once traveled to Spain with a vegetarian, and all she could eat was cheese and bread.

If you are able and willing, be flexible and try different foods. Many countries take great pride in their cooking. To miss ethnic cuisine is to miss culture, whether you like it or not.

20. LGBT

The only queer people are those who don't love anybody. — Rita Mae Brown

It's important to study the social and cultural norms surrounding friendship, dating, homophobia, and dress in the host culture that you are contemplating for study. Does the legal system offer protection or harm when sexual orientation is involved? What is normal for you at home may elicit a different reaction in another country. You could be discriminated against, or at worse, harmed.

See the regional information section of the International Gay and Lesbian Human Rights Commission at iglhrc.org to learn about what is happening in different countries around the world. Also, see the Department of State Country Reports on Human Rights Practices. If you're going to Europe, there is a country-by-country guide at ilga-europe.org.

The International Lesbian and Gay Association at ilga.org is working for the human rights of LGBT people. In the search box, type "State-sponsored Homophobia" for a report on laws prohibiting same sex activity. Type "World Legal Survey" to access a map on international legislation affecting LGBT people.

GETTING STARTED

21. When and how long to go

He travels best that knows when to return. — Thomas More

Historically, the junior year has been the most popular time for students to study abroad, but college students are now going abroad during all phases of their education, even during spring, winter, and summer breaks. It largely depends on academic and personal circumstances.

Every university has its own policies about when and for how long students can study abroad for credit. Your freshmen and senior years may be restricted, and you may not be able to go for longer than a year. It's always best to find out early, so that you can plan accordingly.

The more time you spend completing academic requirements at home, the more limited you are in your choices abroad. For example, if you have already completed your general education courses, then your study abroad courses can only replace major and minor requirements. If you are not getting valuable credit abroad, then you are not maximizing your experience.

Consider the seasons and the calendar also. If you study in Australia from July to November, you will have the summer (December to February in the southern hemisphere) to enjoy afterwards. If you study abroad in Argentina during summer in the United States, it will be winter there and the weather will be cold. The Southern hemisphere is the opposite of the United States.

It's never too early to plan. If you just graduated from high school, think about what you want to get out of a study abroad experience and start looking for a program during your first year. This will help you decide which classes to take and which ones to hold off taking until you go. There are many possibilities, but a traditional plan looks something like this:

Freshman	Gather information from a variety of sources; choose a location and program. Research and apply for scholarships.
Sophomore	Apply to a program, continue to apply for scholarships, and plan your experience.
Junior	Spend the year living and studying abroad. Get to know the culture and the locals. Maximize your experience.
Senior	Finish your degree and integrate your study abroad experience into your life, resume, and career goals.

22. Study abroad program types

Man cannot discover new oceans unless he has the courage to lose sight of the shore. — Andre Gide

Find the office that helps students study abroad, and go there to find out what types of programs are available. If you bypass this step, and go abroad on your own, keep in mind that you will probably have difficulties applying your financial aid and receiving credit for coursework. Colleges may operate their own programs or outsource. If your college does not offer study abroad, you can go through another institution and transfer the credit back. Below are five programs that students commonly use to study abroad:

EXCHANGE

You study at University X, and a student from University X studies at your college. You and the other student pay regular tuition at your own institutions.

This is the least expensive way to study abroad when the tuition cost at the host institution is greater than what you would pay at home. The number of participants is always limited.

DIRECT ENROLL

You apply directly to the institute or university abroad, and enroll in courses available to international students.

This is another inexpensive way to study abroad, but can also be time consuming. Fewer support services usually require more independence, making this option best suited for students already comfortable with international travel. Students are usually responsible for their own housing and transportation. Fluency in the foreign language may be required.

Some advantages include greater flexibility in curriculum and access to hard sciences and other subjects that are more difficult to find in regular study abroad programs. In general, there is a large variety of courses available. You also have more opportunity to befriend students from different nationalities and a high level of immersion in the host culture.

PROGRAM PROVIDER
A company submits the admissions materials on your behalf and makes most arrangements for you (classes, housing, orientation, etc.). Onsite directors and excursions are common. They take care of you and provide explicit instructions when you need do something on your own.

This is the most costly way to study abroad, but there's a strong focus on customer service. It is best suited for those who don't want to travel alone and prefer a high level of support. It is also good for those who don't want to spend time and money planning their excursions, insurance, etc.

CONSORTIUM
Your college has an agreement with a group of programs that belong to different colleges and universities. Alternatively, one program is shared by various colleges and universities. The process may be simple or complex. Arrangements made on your behalf may be minimal or extensive.

This path is usually more expensive than a *direct enroll*, but less than a *program provider*. An extra level of service is generally extended, but it requires you to make many of your own arrangements for courses, housing, transportation, etc.

EXTENSION OF YOUR UNIVERSITY
In this case, your university has an international branch, owns an international program, or sends faculty members abroad for the sole purpose of teaching a group of students. When professors take students abroad for a short period, it's called a *faculty-led program*. This group may travel around or stay put. The cost varies, depending on the location, sponsors, and length of time.

Institutional programs easily meet campus requirements without having to be pre-approved for university credit. Unlike exchanges and direct enroll options, these programs can accommodate large numbers of students. They are well suited for inexperienced travelers.

INTEGRATED VS. ISLAND PROGRAM

An *integrated program* provides a level of structure that enables students to get involved in the local language, community, and culture. Conversely, an *island program* clusters international students within a tight framework that encourages community with other international students, or other American students, rather than locals. They are two completely different experiences so pay attention to this detail.

SHORT-TERM FIELD STUDY

These programs combine class time at the home institution with an international learning experience. Students apply theory to hands-on experiences and reflect critically upon issues and topics.

23. The right program for you

The shoe that fits one person pinches another; there is no recipe for living that suits all cases.
— Carl Gustav Jung

Knowing yourself is the key to finding the right program fit. During my first stint in the Peace Corps, I worked in a remote African village with a population of one thousand. My job was to teach health education. Since I felt comfortable with the people, made some friends, and learned my way around, I had an overall positive experience.

During my second tour in the Corps, I was placed in an urban youth development position in Quito, the capital of Ecuador. While youth development work was a better fit for my vocational goals, it was extremely hard for me to adjust to life in the big city. I ended up asking the Peace Corps if they could reassign me to a small village. They told me that they could do this only if I went back to my work in health education. Consequently, I chose to sacrifice the better-suited job for a smaller location.

Take some time to think about what you want to get out of a study-abroad opportunity. Far too often, students make decisions based on hearsay. One student said it was awesome, so others go too. The ideal study abroad experience will fit your schedule and budget, complement your character, and help you achieve your personal, academic, and career goals.

WHERE TO START?

Iiepassport.org provides an excellent online program directory with over 6000 study abroad programs sponsored by accredited U.S. and foreign institutions. Most study abroad offices have them on hand, and you can purchase them through the Institute of International Education.

The International Handbook of Universities was first published in 1959; this handbook is a good resource for accredited colleges and universities around the world. Published once every two years by Palgrave Macmillan, it is usually available in your study abroad office.

Petersons.com claims the most robust source of college and university information available anywhere.

Study Abroad 2000+ is a 640-page trilingual guide to study abroad opportunities and scholarships, published by UNESCO. Best of all, it's completely free to download.

24. Getting ready to apply

We are always getting ready to live, but never living.— Ralph Waldo Emerson

By now, you should be completed with your research. If you're sure that you've looked at all the options, weighed the pros and cons, and found a program that is a good fit for your academic and personal goals, then start filling out the application materials.

Be truthful. If your GPA isn't up to par, don't exaggerate or mislead. GPAs are never rounded to the nearest tenth (2.75 is not a 3.0). Your chances of getting into a program are greater if you're honest, even if your GPA is a bit lower. Every year students get into serious trouble for lying and cheating.

Spelling and grammatical errors are red flags for many decision makers, so make sure your application is well written, clean, and organized. Include strong references that support your studying abroad. Choose people who see you as a positive ambassador and expect you to have a healthy and safe experience.

There may be several decision makers involved in the application process, but the host institution formally admits you with a letter of acceptance. Depending on the program and country, this may take some time. If you don't hear back within a reasonable period, call your study abroad advisor for updates.

Program fees and profit margins are based on enrollment targets. If a target isn't met, the program must take a loss, cancel, or extend its search for viable candidates. Usually, the first step is to extend, so if you're running late, don't assume that you've missed out.

If applying late, after the deadline, chances are you'll have to rush a number of other tasks (apply late for a passport, obtain a visa, sign up for courses, make sure you have enough financial aid, get recommended and required immunizations, have courses pre-approved, secure housing, purchase your airfare), and more.

The earlier, the better.

LOGISTICAL PLANNING

25. You've been accepted

The original lists were probably carved in stone and represented longer periods of time. They contained things like 'Get More Clay. Make Better Oven' — David Viscott

Congratulations, if you've successfully made it through the application process. Now it's time to start planning.

It's important that you talk to your family before making any final decisions about a study abroad program. Allowing them to be involved in the process will help you in certain aspects of preparation. Don't underestimate the value of their support.

If you don't already have one, apply for your passport right away, as you may need it early in the process to get a visa. You can't get a visa without a passport first.

Sign and return relevant paperwork. This may include a Statement of Responsibility, the payment and refund policy, among other things. Read carefully and make sure you understand everything. Disclose and discuss any pertinent health information and special needs. This is critical to receiving proper support.

If you haven't already done so, select and verify your courses and have them pre-approved to replace academic requirements. Select twice as many as you plan to take, in case of cancellations. Every institution has a different process in place for approving study abroad coursework.

Make sure your financial aid is in order. If not already on file, your host representative may have to fill out a standard consortium agreement certifying that they will not administer Title IV financial aid for you, since it's being administered by your home institution.

Select and secure your housing overseas. It is important that you do not wait until the last minute to find housing, because space is often limited (especially for on-campus housing) and available on a first come first serve basis. The best options will always fill up first.

Read country-specific information from the U.S. Department of State on travel.state.gov and buy a good country guidebook.

Purchase your international airfare, if you already have your passport and don't need a visa. If you need a visa and don't have it yet, then wait.

Purchase an optional International Student ID Card and any insurance not provided by your program.

If you're planning to be gone for more than a semester, give a trustworthy parent, friend, or relative *Power of Attorney* to watch over your financial aid and other assets. Power of Attorney is a legal instrument that delegates lawful and signature authority to another. Forms can be obtained on the Internet or through your lawyer, and are filed in the County Clerk's Office.

26. Get your passport and visa

Education is the passport to the future, for tomorrow belongs to those who prepare for it today.
— Malcolm X

A passport is a form of international identification that verifies your citizenship and other important information needed by immigration. If you don't already have a passport, then you should apply as soon as you know you'll be studying abroad. Processing can take four to eight weeks, although expedited service is available. A U.S. adult passport is valid for ten years. If you already have one, make sure it's valid for at least six months after you will complete your travels abroad.

You can find applications and renewal forms at U.S. postal offices, study abroad offices, courthouses, travel agencies, and travel.state.gov/passport. If you are applying for the first time, and you are at least thirteen years of age, or your passport was issued before you turned sixteen, you must apply in person. You will need to bring two identical passport photos (two by two inches), a photo ID, an original birth certificate or a previous passport, and two blank checks.

Don't forget to sign your passport and fill in the emergency information. It is also wise if a parent or close friend at home has a valid passport while you're away, just in case an emergency comes up that requires immediate travel. If your parent or friend doesn't have a valid passport, there is a same-day passport service available for a legitimate emergency. You must provide proof that you are leaving within three working days to qualify for this service and you typically have to go to a major passport office. It takes about four to six hours.

A visa is an official document, stamp, or seal affixed within your passport, which allows you to enter a foreign country for a particular purpose. A foreign government may issue a visa for tourism, study, or work. If you are a U.S. citizen, you can determine whether you need a visa by visiting the website of the foreign consulate. If you determine you need a visa, apply as soon as possible, usually no earlier than ninety days prior to your program. The process can take anywhere from a few days to several months.

If you're a U.S. citizen traveling to up to ninety days, you may not need a visa in some countries. However, there are other countries where you'll need a visa for any length of time, even a week. Be prepared to have a passport valid for at least six months after your return date, an acceptance letter or enrollment certificate from the host institution, the address where you'll be staying, official verification of your international health insurance, and bank statements that show you have sufficient funds to pay for your stay.

Apply for a passport while applying for your study abroad program. If you need a visa later, then you can either use a visa agency or find the website of your host country's consulate. Look for the student section. Follow directions carefully and double-check everything. Make copies for your records and provide copies of original documents if requested. If your visa requires a visit, make an appointment as soon as possible.

For security reasons, use certified mail when sending important documents. When talking with consular officials in person or on the phone, always ask for their names. When you get your visa, check the information carefully to make sure there are no errors. Don't make travel plans until you have your passport and visa in hand, or until you are sure that you'll have the documents before your departure.

There are other things to keep in mind. Do not block out account numbers on bank statements unless the consulate gives you permission to do so. Staple where it says to staple and glue where it says to glue. Keep your paperwork in the appropriate order. Do not submit scanned photographs; use official passport photos. Follow payment requirements carefully. For example, many consulates will not accept personal checks.

27. Where you will live

I long, as does every human being, to be at home wherever I find myself. — Maya Angelou

Your housing options will vary dramatically, depending on the program, institution, and country. Of all complaints, one of the most frequent is housing, mostly because students don't do enough research beforehand. They don't take time to gather details about a particular housing situation or check student reviews.

A *homestay* usually means room and board with a host family, a great way to acclimate to the culture. *Student housing* usually means residence halls or apartments, which are owned or leased by the school, external provider, or another outside company. *Independent housing* is any kind of accommodation that you find and manage on your own, with directory information.

Be prepared to make a compromise. Your ideal housing may be forty-five minutes away from school, but are you willing to get up early to make the commute? Living with a family can be beneficial to learning the language, but are you willing to sacrifice privacy and space? Keep in mind that photographs in brochures and fliers are often taken with a wide-angle lens, so they look bigger. Space is limited in many parts of the world.

28. Medical preparation

The greatest wealth is health. — Virgil

_____ Visit cdc.gov/travel, sponsored by the National Center for Infectious Diseases. This site provides up-to-date health information about specific travel destinations, including recommended vaccinations and how to avoid getting sick.

_____ Schedule a medical checkup. Develop a personal health strategy with your doctor for the time that you will be away.

_____Update and get copies of your medical records, in case you need them abroad.

_____Get immunized. Do this early; some vaccines like Hepatitis A or B require a series of two or more doses over a six-month period.

_____Get an *International Certificate of Vaccinations* by WHO, if there are immunization restrictions in the countries you'll be visiting. See who.int.

_____Make arrangements to bring a complete supply of medications you take regularly. In addition, bring an extra pair of glasses or contacts in case of damage or loss. Some countries require a letter from your physician if you need to use an inhaler.

_____Check to see that your prescriptions and over-the-counter medications are legal in the countries you'll be visiting. You can usually find this information on the U.S. embassy's website for any country. In Japan, Sudafed, pseudoephedrine, Vicks inhalers, and codeine is illegal for example.

_____Obtain a copy of your prescriptions, and bring the pharmacy statement for how they should be used, in case you're questioned by an immigration officer.

_____Make sure your prescriptions are written for generic versions and not name brands, since name brands may not be available overseas.

_____Keep all prescription medications in their original containers.

_____Document your blood type, allergies, and medical conditions, and carry this documentation with you. Plan to wear a medical identification bracelet or necklace if you have life-threatening allergies or serious illnesses.

_____Put together a starter supply of toiletries, a first aid kit, sunscreen, insect repellent, tissue paper, and a mosquito net (if going to a tropical area with malaria).

_____Pick out two or three doctors and a hospital, in the event that you become ill or need to get medical attention and care.

_____Indicate your personal health needs on your medical and housing forms so that the program administrators can better support you. Don't forget to include allergies, dietary needs, challenges, and phobias. If you have a phobia of dogs, you shouldn't be placed with a family that has one.

_____Review the consular information issued by other governments, to obtain a broader, worldwide perspective: Australia smartraveller.gov.au, Canada voyage.gc.ca, Great Britain fco.gov.uk.

_____Take precautions to avoid getting sick. This will depend greatly on where you will be living and studying. Read destination information on the CDC website (wwwnc.cdc.gov/Travel) and follow it.

_____Plan to carry with you appropriate medications and equipment for emergency self-treatment, specific to the area(s) you are visiting, such as a snakebite kit in remote areas.

29. Shopping for your flight

A good traveler has no fixed plans, and is not intent on arriving. — Lao Tzu

Check a variety of sources and purchase your flight well in advance. After you purchase your ticket, don't worry too much about price changes. My Yapta (https://my.yapta.com) monitors ticketed flights. When savings are significant enough to re-ticket, they alert you. Their website claims an average net savings of $260 after airline change fees.

Flying on a Tuesday, Wednesday, or Thursday can be cheaper than other days of the week. Consider rate differences at neighboring airports and red-eye flights that depart late in the evening or early in the morning. If you're going to Europe, you can use London or another gateway city as a hub, then take a budget airline or train to your final destination.

Consolidators work if you are flexible on your dates and live in or close to an international airport. They buy unsold tickets in bulk, directly from airlines and then resell them to individuals at a discount. Check the Sunday travel sections of big newspapers like the *Chicago Tribune* or the *NY Times*. If you're buying late, look into agencies and websites that specialize in last minute travel.

Always purchase airfare using a credit card, in case your travel agent or airline goes bankrupt. Under the Fair Credit Billing Act (FCBA), Visa, MasterCard, and American Express purchases receive substantially more protections than cash and checks. Ask your credit card company for details.

There's more to consider than financial. Does your student visa require an onward or roundtrip plane ticket (i.e. China)? Sometimes consulates will not issue a visa and border control won't let you through without one. Are you on a scholarship that requires you to use a U.S. carrier? Is your ticket refundable? If not, do you have trip insurance? What are the baggage limitations and excess fees? Depending on the airport, airlines can be very strict.

A round-trip ticket is usually the cheapest way of flying with fixed dates to and from the destination. A flexible round-trip ticket is one with a return date that you can set up later. A round-the-world ticket includes a sequence of tickets to take you to multiple destinations at a discount, but you have to book everything in advance. Go westbound to avoid redeye flights; go eastbound for overnighters.

Sometimes I fly into one destination and fly home from another, and it turns out to be cheaper than flying to and from the same destination. Pisa and Bologna are not far from Florence, Italy, but tickets into these airports can cost hundreds less.

When searching for international airfare, kayak.com, studentuniverse.com, and skyskanner.com are good choices. To find deals from budget airlines, take a look at whichbudget.com or flycheapo.com.

Additional Resources

Flight tracker—flightaware.com
Frequent flyer miles—webflyer.com
Meals—airlinemeals.net
Seats—seatguru.com
Sleeping in airports—sleepinginairports.net
Unclaimed baggage—unclaimedbaggage.com

30. International ID

Half the fun of travel is the esthetic of lostness. — Ray Bradbury

To buy or not to buy an International ID card? Most foreign universities will give you a student identification card. However, there are several commercial cards that come with benefits.

The *International Student Identification Card (ISIC)* can be purchased online, through various travel agencies and many study abroad offices. It provides valuable discounts in the United States and more than a hundred other countries, including discounts on airfare and a mobile communications package. It also provides some basic health insurance as well as emergency evacuation and repatriation of remains. Finally, it offers some travel insurance for lost documents, baggage and delays, as well as 24-hour assistance.

iNext is focused more on insurance than discounts around the world. It offers several different supplemental and comprehensive levels of coverage to choose from. All iNext cards are valid for a full year from the date of purchase anywhere in the world outside of the United States. Anyone over the age of thirteen years can purchase an iNext card and eligibility is not restricted to student or faculty status like it is with ISIC.

The International Student Exchange Card (ISECard) offers students international discounts, reimbursement of insurance deductibles per occurrence, worldwide assistance, and airline bankruptcy protection.

31. Insurance coverage

Precaution is better than cure. — Edward Coke

Be sure to have adequate health and emergency insurance that will cover you internationally. In some cases, it may be provided by your home institution, and in other cases, it may be included with your fees to a program provider. It may also be covered by the government of the country you are visiting, after you register for classes and pay your fees. Wherever your insurance comes from, make sure it's enough.

Medicare and Medicaid don't cover services outside of the United States, and your regular health insurance company may not provide sufficient travel-specific coverage and limits. An emergency medical evacuation can cost over $100,000, far beyond what is *customary* and *reasonable* according to most insurance companies. In addition to coverage, you should look at your financial resources and whether or not you need a direct-pay service or you can apply for reimbursement after you submit receipts.

One man, whose appendix ruptured while he was in Europe, was relying on the insurance provided by ISIC. Because ISIC does not pay hospitals directly, and he didn't have enough money to pay the bill at the hospital, they held his passport and wouldn't let him leave. Luckily, a friend was able to collect enough money to pay the bill and have him released. While he did get ISIC to reimburse him later on, the situation that he forwent in the hospital was dreadful. If your insurance company doesn't pay hospitals directly, then make sure that you have a substantial emergency fund available and accessible by a third party.

There are many different insurance companies with advantages and limitations. At a minimum, you need major medical, medical evacuation, and repatriation insurance. You may also consider trip interruption insurance to protect your investment, in case something prevents you from going or requires you to return early. It's also not a bad idea to consider security evacuation for natural disasters, outbreak of war, and terrorist attacks; or else you will depend on your local U.S. embassy. If you are traveling to an area where kidnapping or terrorism is common, consider kidnapping and terrorism insurance.

You can shop for insurance and compare rates through many websites. However, purchase directly from the company, not from a third party. If you purchase from a third party that goes under, then you'll need to stand in line with all the creditors, which might prove difficult from across the ocean. Also, don't fall for a great price at the sacrifice of good quality and reputation. Read the fine print, especially exclusion clauses and look at the amount of coverage. The following minimum coverage is necessary, but I recommend more:

Medical Expenses – 100K or more per incident

Prescription Drugs – 80% to 100% coverage

Emergency Medical Evacuation – 100K (per occurrence) with flexibility in accommodating different needs, such as low altitude flight capacity for head injuries. For remote locations, consider up to 250K.

Repatriation of Remains – 50K

24-hour traveler assistance hotline

Emergency Family Reunion – $2,500

Some mental health benefits

Coverage for your return and subsequent care in the United States

---

For most non-emergency consultations, if your provider is out-of-network with your insurance company, then you'll need to get an itemized receipt and present it for reimbursement. Since medical consultations are more affordable in other countries, paying up front is usually not a problem for minor issues. Note, many insurance policies will overlap. If you have more than one insurer, know which is *primary* and *secondary* and what that means for your particular situation.

32. Packing right

When preparing to travel, lay out all your clothes and all your money. Then take half the clothes and twice the money. — Susan Heller

What and how to pack isn't as easy as it looks. The best way is to prepare a checklist of items you think you'll need and narrow it down to no more than you can carry by yourself at one time. A small suitcase with wheels, a large travel backpack, and a daypack should be sufficient for everything. After you've packed, carry your luggage around the block to see if it's too heavy. If you can't endure long, then repack. Learn the art and science of traveling light at <u>onebag.com</u>.

GENERAL TIPS
Use ugly, weird, or worn durable bags that can be easily distinguished from the luggage of others. Put identification tags on your luggage inside and out and photograph it. Use only TSA-approved locks, which can be opened by the Transportation Security Administration with universal master keys. Don't wrap gifts, unless you don't mind if they are unwrapped by security.

Keep in mind that most fruits, vegetables and animal products are not transportable across international borders. Don't bring things that you can easily purchase abroad, like food and toiletries, unless you have some favorite hard-to-find soap or cream that you won't be able to live without.

Remember, you'll probably be bringing home more than you take. So it's a good idea to get an extra nylon bag or backpack that you can shape into a ball, pack in one of your other bags, and fill up with souvenirs and other goodies when you return. Alternatively, you can buy a bag abroad, but it might be harder to find exactly what you want.

Plan for all possible weather conditions and activities. I tend to dress in layers and wear dark-colored clothing that doesn't show dirt and doesn't need to be ironed. If I'm not going to be abroad for a long time, I bring old clothes to sleep in and lounge around the house, and then I give them away when I leave. This frees up space in my luggage for souvenirs and gifts.

Bring a laptop to access the Internet, do your homework, listen to music, call home, store your digital pictures, watch movies, and more. Electronic devices are less expensive in the United States, so it's best to bring your own devices. Consider insuring these devices through your homeowner's insurance, and backup your data in a separate location.

Note, there are many items that are illegal to take on a plane, and rules can change frequently. Nowadays, you can't even carry on a tube of toothpaste unless it's three ounces or less and in a one-quart clear plastic bag, and you can't carry a bottle of water through airport security. Consult the Transportation Security Administration for up-to-date information: tsa.gov/public. Be prepared to take electronics out of your bag, as well as remove loose clothing and shoes when you go through security.

Most electronic devices like hair dryers are better purchased abroad. If you insist on bringing them from home, determine the voltage and outlets, and purchase an adapter and possibly a converter if needed. An adapter is just a small device that fits over your plug and into the outlet. It doesn't change voltage, so if you use it without a converter, it can fry things such as radios, hairdryers, and other voltage-dependent devices. A converter changes the voltage, but don't forget to flip the switch on your appliance (if applicable).

In the United States, most equipment operates with 110 volts, but in Europe, it's 220 volts. Modern laptops have built-in converters.

Don't take anything valuable that you don't need and are comfortable leaving at home. In some places, I've heard of thieves cutting off fingers to get to diamond rings.

Vacuum-sealed space bags can keep things fresh and save a lot of space, too. I use them just to keep my clothes smelling nice.

CARRY-ON BAG

Pack your carry-on bag as if you were living out of it for at least two or three nights. If your luggage is lost or flights are delayed, you will want to brush your teeth and change your socks and underwear. Also, be sure to carry on anything that you can't live without, as well as valuable items such as plane tickets, your passport, plastic cards, birth certificates, health records, host letters, and certifications. Don't carry on seemingly harmless items that could be perceived as weapons.

You should have the following:

_____Passport, visa, and plane tickets

_____Photocopies of your passport and plane tickets (put a few copies in different bags and give a copy to someone at home). You can photograph your passport and store it on your cell phone as well.

_____International Certificate of Vaccinations

_____Health insurance card and benefits information

_____Home university ID card (unless you're getting ISIC)

_____One or two ATM cards (must be numeric for checking accounts, not savings; most popular are PLUS and CIRRUS)

_____ One or two credit cards (Visa, MasterCard, AMEX)

_____$100 cash for emergency use

_____Your devices, extra cords, and a solar charger comes in handy

_____Address, directions, and map to where you're going from your point of arrival and information about who to call in case you get lost or there is some emergency. Download offline google maps to your phone also.

_____A list of phone numbers (emergency contacts, home advisors, health insurance, home doctors, host advisors, U.S. embassy, and local 911) and card numbers (debit, credit, ID) with how to report if they are lost or stolen. If you can encode this information, it's better. Just don't forget how to decode! Note, 800 & toll-free numbers won't work abroad. Leave a copy of your lists with a trusted individual at home. Alternatively, you can make front and back copies of all your cards.

_____ Your choice of doctor and hospital on-site as well as your blood type, allergies, and medical conditions

_____ A list of what is in all your suitcases in case lost or stolen, so you can make an insurance claim

_____Extra passport photos (for IDs and emergencies)

_____Money belt to put under your clothing and carry your credit card, ATM card, phone numbers, cash, and a copy of your passport

_____Waist pack or fanny pack to carry like a purse when appropriate

_____If you're checking your other bag, then you need enough essentials for two to three nights of lost luggage.

_____Prescriptions and over-the-counter medications for at least a month (if applicable), including eyeglasses or contacts. Carry all medications in their original containers; mixing them in one container will likely confuse customs officers and cause headaches for you.

_____Extra pair of eyeglasses or contact lenses

These items are optional:

_____A good travel guide for the area with maps

_____A small bilingual dictionary with phrases

_____Rail Passes, ISIC, Hostel Card, etc.

_____iPod or another music player

_____USB flash drive (to save work for printing in a lab)

_____Batteries and chargers for any equipment you have

_____Electrical adapters if needed (to fit electrical outlet). These come in handy for all your devices.

_____Electrical converter if needed (to convert electrical voltage, usually from 110 to 220)

_____Addresses, photos of family and friends, in case your device is lost or stolen

CHECKED LUGGAGE
Usually, you can check one suitcase for international flights, with size and weight restrictions that you must adhere to in order to avoid hefty fines.

_____7 socks and underwear

_____1 bathing suit

_____3 of each kind type of clothing that you wear often (t-shirts, shorts, slacks, skirts, dresses, long sleeve shirts, short sleeve shirts, sweaters, etc.), according to your personal preference and style. Keep in mind that you can buy clothes abroad, too.

_____1 coat and jacket (waterproof and wind-resistant)

_____1 travel umbrella (or plan to buy one abroad)

_____2 pajamas

_____1 pair of each kind of shoes you plan to wear more than once (walking, running, dressy, flip-flop, casual, etc.)

_____2-3 plastic bags for wet or dirty clothes

_____1 starter supply of toiletries (toothbrush, toothpaste, bath sponge, fast-drying towel, dental floss, creams, makeup, tampons, pads, razors, deodorant, insect repellent, sunscreen)

_____1 tweezer and nail kit (file, cutter, etc.)

_____1 hair brush and comb

_____pocket knife with a bottle opener, corkscrew, and can opener (all-in-one, don't put in carry-on bag)

_____small flashlight

_____first aid medical kit for your particular needs

_____sewing kit

_____multivitamins (I take vitamin B for jetlag)

_____your preferred pain reliever

_____sun glasses and a hat (to protect from sun or cold)

_____hostel sleep sack (a sheet folded and hemmed)

_____notebook, weekly planner, pens, pencils (minimum, since you can buy abroad)

_____mosquito net (if going to malaria-prone area)

_____small gifts (for host family, friends)

_____pack of cards, this book, a journal

_____an extra day bag or backpack for school and light travel

_____water filter (in undeveloped countries where water isn't potable, or if you're doing a lot of outdoor excursions where you cannot or don't want to boil water)

33. Seek knowledge

Live as if you were to die tomorrow. Learn as if you were to live forever.
— Mahatma Gandhi

Learn as much as possible about your destination. Start with a good guidebook on your host country, then the U.S. embassy's website. If you're traveling to Europe, spend some time on the European Union's website: europa.eu. This is an outstanding resource with lots of information about the laws, structure, countries, and history.

Get informed about U.S. issues, foreign policy, and world affairs by reading major newspapers online. Great Decisions is America's largest discussion program on world affairs. The Department of State also publishes country information on U.S. bilateral relations with history regarding U.S. assistance and representation.

If you're going to be living with a family, then you may want to give them a gift when you arrive. First, find out if gifts are appropriate, and how they should be presented. In some Asian countries, the wrapping is more important than what's inside. It is a good idea to pick out something that is unavailable in the host country, which represents where you are from, and isn't heavy or bulky.

Have a general idea about where major cities are located and what they represent to people. Know your host country's relations with other countries also, especially neighbors. You should develop a cultural "common sense" like whether it is appropriate to ask questions during lectures, rest your feet on another table or chair, eat during class time, arrive late or leave early, chew gum, send and text messages. Learn more at cyborlink.com, a good resource for international business etiquette, manners, and cross-cultural communication.

34. Other things to do before you go

Motivation is what gets you started. Habit is what keeps you going. — Jim Rohn

_____REGISTRATION. Register with the Department of State in the countries you'll be visiting (name, passport number, dates, and location) via travelregistration.state.gov if you're a U.S. citizen or a permanent resident. Otherwise, register with your country's equivalent. Anytime you plan to stay in another country, you should register in case of an emergency.

_____ORIENTATIONS. Attend recommended or required pre-departure orientations organized by your home university.

_____PAYING BILLS. Make arrangements for your bills, either paying online or asking a family member for help.

_____VOTING ABROAD. Make arrangements to vote from abroad, by absentee ballot. Visit the Federal Voting Assistance Program: fvap.gov.

_____GRADUATE SCHOOL TESTS. Arrange to take the GRE, LSAT, GMAT, or MCAT, if you plan to apply for graduate school.

_____CLASSES AT HOME. Arrange to register for the semester when you return. Drop any classes you may have registered for while you will be away.

_____HOUSING AT HOME. Arrange to secure housing for the semester that you return to your home campus. Also, don't forget to cancel any home-campus housing contracts for the time that you'll be away.

_____RAIL PASS. If you're going to buy a rail pass for Europe, do it before you leave. You can't buy one in Europe.

_____UPDATE ADDRESS. Make sure your addresses with schools, banks, and service companies are updated to your permanent address, where someone is checking your mail while you are away.

_____RENEW PLASTIC CARDS. You don't want to find yourself with an expired passport, driver's license, health insurance card, ATM card, or credit card.

_____NOTIFY BANKS. Notify your banks when you will be traveling and where, so they don't put a false fraud-alert on your cards and stop service. Nowadays, suspicious activity often triggers automatic deactivation. You may also consider purchasing identity fraud protection.

_____EMERGENCY NUMBERS. Carry your passport or a copy of your passport AND emergency telephone numbers at all times. This includes

Overseas Citizens Services: 1-888-407-4747 (U.S.) and 202-501-4444 (overseas) for death, arrest, detention, robbery, missing persons, and other crisis involving American citizens after hours. You can go to usembassy.state.gov to locate your host country and write down the embassy contact information, local 911 number, and other emergency numbers.

____Wear comfortable clothing for your trip. Dress in layers in case you get too hot or cold on the flight. Bring a cardigan if you're not wearing one. Don't wear jewelry and don't carry metal in your pockets, to prevent having to take it off and out during airport screening.

____Put all official documentation, personal information, and valuables with your carry-on items. In addition to what's on your carry-on packing list, think about adding enough clothing and toiletries for two to three days, in case your checked luggage is lost or stolen.

____Map your final destination (i.e. hotel, school, family), and figure out how you're going to get there, before you get on the plane. Have a backup plan if this fails.

____Have the map, address, and phone number of school and family accessible in your carry-on bag.

____Tag all your luggage inside and out, in case of loss.

____Bring enough cash for a few days, in case of a problem.

____Bring something to do on the plane and during layovers.

____Bring snacks, especially if you tend to get hungry between meals.

____Double-check your departure dates and times, paying careful attention to AM and PM. One student I know missed her flight because she thought it was PM when it was AM.

____Call at least 72 hours in advance to confirm your flights. Sometimes there are cancellations and changes.

____Check in early to avoid long lines and last-minute crowds, and subsequently missed flights.

____Never leave your bags unattended and don't carry or transport items for others. Keep a careful watch on your bags.

____Register valuables with the U.S. Customs station at your international airport of departure. Keep the certificates.

____Leave your itinerary with someone. Say goodbye to people you love and be sure to have their email and phone.

____Last but not least, don't forget your passport!

35. Airports, planes, immigration

Most travel is best of all in the anticipation or the remembering; the reality has more to do with losing your luggage. — Regina Nadelson

Once you get to the airport, you can expect to check in, drop off your luggage, and go through a screening process with your carry-on bags and personal items. Anything that should be removed (shoes, blazers, jackets, belts, etc.) must be placed on the conveyor belt and you'll be asked to walk through a metal detector, or some other big machine that blows air at you. If there's a detection, you'll get a secondary screening with a handheld device and possibly a pat down.

On the plane, you can sit back and relax as much as possible in the cramped seating. If you have a layover, then you'll need to change planes in the airport. If you end up missing a flight because one of the planes didn't make it on time, then the airline representative will put you on the next available flight. If you have to spend the night, ask about hotel and food vouchers. Airlines will usually pay if it is their fault. They will not pay for bad weather or anything out of their control.

You should be able to get a meal or two on most international flights, and watch movies, listen to music, or play games. Unless you're in first class, you probably won't sleep well. You can buy a neck pillow, or there are often wings on your seat that fold in and keep your head from flopping around. Be sure to have a pen, your passport number, and the address where you are staying for any immigration paperwork you will have to fill out.

When you arrive, you will have to go through customs with your passport. If you don't have a visa, and you aren't planning to get one at the airport, then you should keep the words "study" and "work" out of your vocabulary. "Tourism" is a great word and it's true. Keep any immigration papers in a safe place for your return trip.

After you exit customs, there will be a place where you can pick up your baggage. If your baggage doesn't arrive, then file a claim. All airlines have procedures to search for lost baggage, and when found, your bags are delivered to you at wherever it is you're staying. Alternatively, you can pick them up. Most bags are found, and it turns out to be an inconvenience rather than a loss.

HEALTH AND SAFETY

36. Safety in study abroad

Safety is something that happens between your ears, not something you hold in your hands.
— Jeff Cooper

Although you may be prepared with lots of good information, it's easy to let down your guard once you are familiar and comfortable with the territory. The euphoria of being in a foreign country, combined with a new version of you, can erect a false sense of security.

Petty theft is by far the most common crime against students who study abroad. This includes bag snatchers and pickpockets who rob unsuspecting tourists. I was eating in a Barcelona café when a woman's purse was stolen. The video surveillance caught the man on tape, but cleverly, his face was hidden by a cowboy hat.

Use a money belt under your clothing to carry your passport, cards, and cash. Don't expose large sums of cash. Leave expensive or sentimental possessions at home. The less you have to carry, the less you will worry about. Don't act like a tourist, but a local. When strangers start asking you for directions, you're probably on the right track.

Other crimes that occur are alcohol-related or have to do with poor decision-making and bad luck. Limit your alcohol consumption to keep your awareness and judgment intact, and don't leave your drink unattended. Date rape drugs are popular all over the world, and are used intentionally to rob and rape people. Be vigilant and never let down your guard.

When I was in the Peace Corps, a young man who finished his two-year service before me was traveling in South Africa. One night, he went to a bar and decided to stay late rather than walk back to the hotel with his friends. He went missing and was found murdered in an alley nearby. His glasses, boots, and wallet were stolen. What a sad story.

Risk, with balance, is necessary and healthy for full enjoyment of life. We take a risk every time we get into a car, train, or plane. What we have to do is be mature enough to understand the risks associated with our behaviors. We should then engage in behaviors because we believe the benefits outweigh the risks rather than feeling immune to misfortune.

Review host country information through the U.S. Department of State at travel.state.gov. This will give you an overview of immigration practices, political disturbances, health conditions, crime and security, and unstable activities. It will also tell you if there are any alerts or warnings for the country. *Travel alerts* are issued for short-term events that you should know about. These may include strikes, demonstrations, or disturbances; virus and flu outbreaks; or evidence of an elevated risk. A *travel warning* is a notice recommending that Americans not travel to particular country.

Know where it is safe and not safe to go at all times. Understand the emergency protocols for your program, and carry an emergency card. Never go out on your own without money, identification, and the addresses and phone numbers of your residence. Be sure to also carry the phone numbers of your leaders and fellow students, not just in the address book on your phone. You should know how to contact your local police and get to a hospital in the event of a medical emergency.

If you're lost, don't whip out a map on the street. Stop for a coffee and get your bearings discretely. Understand how public transportation works and what is safe. Don't wear flashy, risqué, or expensive-looking clothing. Stay in populated areas, avoid crowds, and please don't sleep in public places. Lock your doors and windows when you're home and when you're away; thieves are more audacious in other countries.

During national emergencies, phone lines and internet may go down. Good program leaders establish a communication tree and buddy system with a primary and secondary meeting place. When going away for vacation, make sure the right people know where you're going and how to contact you. Watch your bags and don't be a courier for someone, unless you know the person well and the contents of the package.

Know the local laws, including traffic and pedestrian rules; never assume it is the same as it is back home. Also, don't forget to look both ways when crossing streets. Students have died crossing the streets in London, looking the wrong way and stepping in front of a vehicle.

Stay away from strikes and other demonstrations, especially from tear gas. Don't share your political views with reporters. Avoid American hangouts and large English-speaking groups of people walking around the city. It's better to split up into smaller groups.

For more study abroad safety information, the best resource you will find is globaled.us/safeti.

37. Coping with Jet lag

I refer to jet lag as 'jet-psychosis' — there's an old saying that the spirit cannot move faster than a camel. — Spalding Gray

Jet lag is a disruption of the circadian rhythm—the body's 24-hour inner clock—caused by a change in time zone. If you fly from the United States to France, you miss a night. Although midnight registers on your inner clock, your outer clock reads early in the morning. This means that when the country is asleep, you may feel hungry and energetic. When the country is awake, you may feel exhausted.

Symptoms of jetlag include fatigue, insomnia, irritation of the eyes, nose, or ears, swollen limbs, headaches, dehydration, lightheadedness, and bowel irregularity. You may also feel irritable, aloof, and disoriented. The best way to deal with jetlag is to get lots of rest before you leave. Eat well and take vitamins (especially vitamin B). Dress comfortably so you can relax.

When on the plane, set your watch to the time of your final destination. Avoid alcohol and stay hydrated with lots of water. You should also avoid food and drinks with high sodium content so that you don't swell. Stretch and walk around on the plane frequently, if you can. Avoid crossing your legs at the knees and ankles. Yawn or chew gum to pop pressure buildup in your ears.

When you arrive, start operating on local time right away. This means staying awake the rest of the day. Exercise to increase your energy levels. Most of all, be patient with yourself and you'll adjust.

38. Getting medical care abroad

Never go to a doctor whose office plants have died. — Erma Bombeck

Doctors in other countries do not undergo the same type of education that they do in the United States. This isn't to say they are better or worse, but their approach may be different. For this reason, make a list of physicians and hospitals before you leave, or get a list from the embassy after you arrive in the host country. Then decide where to go for something minor versus major. If you become seriously ill or injured, a U.S. consular officer can help you locate medical services, as well as contact family members.

If you are not going to be gone for more than a semester, it's a good idea to get enough prescription medications to last your entire trip. Leave them in their original containers and keep a copy of the prescription on hand. Put them in your carry-on bag, not your checked luggage. Possession of certain drugs without a prescription may violate local laws. Also, bring syringes or other types of instruments that you use to administer your drugs, with a note from your physician. In some developing countries, medical personnel still reuse needles and syringes.

Stick with major in-country pharmacies. Try to avoid small kiosks that may acquire medications suspiciously. Call the embassy for advice about which pharmacies they trust for their employees. As you might expect, the Food and Drug Administration cannot assure the content or quality of pharmaceuticals sold outside of the United States, so you take them at your own risk. Personally, I've never had a problem with a prescription medication that I received overseas, but I've also never acquired them from illegitimate sources.

Wherever you go, it's important that you understand the health care system. The most efficient health care systems belong to Singapore, Hong Kong SAR, Italy, Japan, and South Korea; the United States ranks 44 out of 51 on the list.[7]

---

[7] Bloomberg, Most Efficient Health Care 2014: Countries. Accessed on April 1, 2019. http://www.bloomberg.com/visual-data/best-and-worst/most-efficient-health-care-countries.

One interesting study conducted by Ellen Nolte and Martin McKee of the London School of Hygiene and Tropical Medicine compared the trends in preventable deaths among industrialized nations. They rated France, Japan and Australia best and the United States worst in preventable deaths due to treatable conditions.[8]

You may be surprised to receive better care abroad than you otherwise would at home. One professor I knew took a very serious fall in Italy while she was leading a study abroad program. Her hospitalization was immediate and high quality. In the end, it didn't cost her anything.

When I relocated to Indiana, I could not find a doctor who would accept me as a new patient. My health was good; I just needed a primary care physician. In one particular case, the nurse took all my personal information to ask the doctor if he would accept me. Three days later, I received a phone call that he would not.

In the Peace Corps, I often had to treat myself for illnesses that I would normally see a doctor about. This is because I wasn't able to obtain optimal health care in my remote African village. If you're in a remote location, I highly recommend, *Where There is No Doctor: A Village Health Care Handbook* by David Werner, Carol Thuman, and Jane Maxwell. It is excellent for identifying and treating both common and rare illnesses.

If you're studying in a rural location, it is very important that you have a good medical evacuation provider as well. Imagine being in a remote area of Costa Rica when you start having severe stomach pain and need to have your appendix removed promptly. If there is no one who can perform a safe surgery for you in a timely manner, then you could die. If you allow an unqualified doctor or primitive health center to perform your surgery, then

----

[8]The Commonwealth Fund, Press Release. New York, NY, September 23, 2011. http://www.commonwealthfund.org/publications/press-releases/2011/sep/us-ranks-last-on-preventable-deaths

you could also die. A good medical evacuation service would have you air-lifted in a timely manner.

Medical practices vary widely in other countries. My dentist in Africa gave me vodka to swish around in my mouth before he checked my aching wisdom teeth. When I sprained my ankle, I happened to stumble upon a traditional healer who rubbed the fat of a boa constrictor on my joint and squeezed it fiercely. He claimed that by massaging my ankle with the boa fat, it would swell up and therefore heal faster.

Consider joining the International Association of Medical Assistance to Travelers, at iamat.org. It's free, but they ask for a donation.

39. Road awareness

At work at play, let safety lead the way. — Unknown

The number one cause of death among U.S. citizens abroad is auto accidents. While accidents happen all over the world, there is a greater risk in developing nations, with deteriorating road infrastructure and regulatory systems and irregular and corrupt law enforcement. In fact, the rate of road deaths in low- and middle-income countries is almost double that of high-income countries, and it's getting worse.

The majority of victims are not occupants of cars, but rather the pedestrians, motorcyclists, and bicyclists that ride beside them. This is because there are no consequences for driving without a license or insurance, or for driving erratically. Drivers are not motivated by law, but rather by how many trips they can make, and thus how much money they can earn in a day. Vehicles are old and not maintained to U.S. standards, and there may be no emergency transportation.

When I was living in Quito, my landlord was hit by a car and killed while walking home after paying her electric bill. She was about seventy years old. It was a difficult and sad moment for me as I liked her a lot. I had to move out of the house, find another place to live, attend her funeral, and offer my condolences, all with very little Spanish language skills. Today, you can find blue hearts all over the streets of Quito where someone died in an accident. The locals paint them to raise awareness and promote safe driving.

For information about road safety, visit the Association for Safe International Road Travel at asirt.org and Sara's Wish Foundation at saraswish.org. In 1996, Sara Wish and three classmates were killed in a fatal bus crash while participating in the University of Pittsburgh's Semester at Sea Program. The Sara Wish Foundation promotes travel safety standards around the globe.

40. Emergencies

One of the true tests of leadership is the ability to recognize a problem before it becomes an emergency. — Arnold H. Glasgow

Register with the U.S. Department of State shortly before you depart. The Smart Traveler Enrollment Program (STEP) is a free service provided to U.S. citizens and nationals who are traveling to a foreign country. It will help you and your family in the event of a personal or national emergency. Go to step.state.gov to get started.

The Overseas Citizens Services (OCS) of the Bureau of Consular Affairs is responsible for the whereabouts and general welfare of U.S. citizens who are overseas. American Citizens Services and Crisis Management (ACS), is a branch of the OCS that assists Americans with many kinds of medical, financial, and legal emergencies. During business hours, call 1-888-407-4747 or 317-472-2328. For after-hour emergencies, call 202-647-4000.

An emergency is an unstable situation, a very stressful event, or a traumatic change in someone's life. Pre-planned responses to a medical emergency, political situation, terrorist attack, natural disaster, legal issue, robbery, assault, and accident-illness-death of people at home can go a long way in helping you prepare for the worst. Emergencies require swift response, and in some cases, response time is a matter of life and death.

Develop awareness. Pay attention to signs and signals. Read the news on a daily basis and know what's happening in the city, country, and world around you. Information increases the odds of your identifying a problem before it hits you, but also avoiding it altogether. Don't forget, knowledge is power; so seek it diligently. It reduces fear and builds confidence. It helps us to manage our behavior toward a positive outcome.

If anything newsworthy happens in your host country, you should quickly get in touch with people at home. When an earthquake hit China, we had a group of students on tour, scheduled to be in Beijing. They did not communicate their safety to anyone at home because they figured that everyone realized they were 960 miles from the epicenter. Meanwhile, frantic parents were calling our office because the media had already announced 10,000 people dead. Can you imagine?

As you think through how to respond to different emergencies, ask yourself if your plan is realistic. If your plan relies on the use of telecommunication devices and electricity in the event of a serious earthquake, for example, then it's probably not going to work. A good plan will get you out of danger, help you find people, and help people find you.

41. Pickpockets and robbery

Poverty is the mother of crime. — Marcus Aurelius

Prevent pickpocketing by keeping your money out of sight and carefully watching your possessions when out and about. Put most of your cash, plastic cards, and passport or copy in a flat pouch tied snuggly around your waist, under your clothing. Put spending money in an inside zipped pocket of your daypack or purse. When you need more money, go to a restroom and move some from the pouch to your daypack or purse. Never carry or stash large sums of cash in the same place. Small purses that hang around the neck from a cord can be easily slit and stolen.

To prevent pickpocketing or theft of your daypack or purse, wear it in a way that people can't grab it and run away. I wear my daypack in front when in crowded places. If you're carrying a wallet, keep it in a front pocket that buttons or zips. Put valuables in zipped pockets that you can close with a safety pin. Don't hang your purse over your shoulder, but rather crisscross it over your chest. Carry your bag or purse on the opposite side of bicycles and vehicles. Never put your purse or bag down in a restaurant or anywhere in public.

Thieves are very sneaky and often attack from behind. My ex-husband and I were in an overly crowded market when someone managed to slip in between he and I, meanwhile his partner pushed everybody in the crowd from behind. We all fell forward like dominos, and when we exited the crowd, my husband's wallet was gone. There was only a dollar in his wallet, but all his identification cards were stolen and he had to spend a lot of time and money getting replacements.

Petty theft is sophisticated in countries typically visited by U.S. students. Pickpockets and bag-snatchers work in pairs. One distracts and the other discretely steals. This is common and easy for thieves to pull off, especially in airports and train stations.

Be careful about children and beggars asking for money. If you want to help people, have loose change in your pocket, but don't take out your wallet since they can grab it and run or discretely follow you and steal it when your guard is down.

Not only do you have to safe keep your money outside, but also inside if you are staying in hotels or living with other people. While it may be easy to blame the cleaning staff, most cases of theft in hotels or apartments can be linked to roommates, friends, and partners of roommates. Yes, as disheartening as it is, they may steal from you, especially if it's easy to get the money while shifting the blame. Don't leave your cash lying around; keep it hidden, even from the unsuspecting.

When you need a good place to store extra cash, think about the layout of your living area or hotel room and where a thief would be least likely to look. Some apartments, schools, and hotels have safes, but safes are often targeted and stolen. Here are a few places to stash cash temporarily:

- In a piece of newspaper, taped to the bottom of a drawer or chair.
- In a sock, inside a bag of dirty clothes (don't accidently wash it).
- In a plastic container in your refrigerator, making it look like old leftovers that nobody wants.
- In the fireplace, as long as it's not functional and you don't forget it's there.
- In a book on a shelf, only if you have lots of books. Also, tape it so it doesn't fall out.
- In the bathroom, in the middle of a toilet paper roll.
- In the medicine cabinet or in a bag of personal toiletries.
- In a photo album, behind some pictures, inside a couch cushion.
- In a pile of graded papers and notes.

Know the local ATM scams. A skimmer, illegally mounted to the front of the card slot, can read ATM card numbers and transmit the information to criminals. A keypad or a hidden wireless camera, which look like a leaflet holder, can record your pin. Avoid these scams by carefully screening the machine before you use it; card slots and key pads shouldn't protrude outwards. Shield your hand when entering your pin, so that cameras can't catch it on tape. These highly skilled thieves can copy cards and use your pin numbers to quickly withdraw large amounts of cash.

There are also digital pickpockets. These thieves have built radio frequency identification (RFID) scanners that electronically steal people's account information embedded on RFID enabled cards. Then, they create duplicate cards and go shopping. This happened to me once, and in a matter of a week, the thieves stole over $8,000. It started with a small charge, to see if the card worked and to see if we were watching. Then they charged large amounts of money as quickly as possible. I had to file a police report and claim with my bank, but eventually I was able to get the money back from insurance. Now I carry my cards in a RFID card protector case, which blocks the signals.

If you get pickpocketed or robbed while abroad, don't panic. First, contact your financial institutions to cancel your cards, and ask one of the three credit reporting companies to initiate a fraud alert. This makes it harder for an identity thief to open more accounts in your name. The alert lasts ninety days but you can renew it. Then, go to the local police station to file a police report. You will need this report to get your passport replaced and to file any claims with your insurance company for stolen goods. It also proves to creditors that you were diligent if there is ever an investigation. With a report in hand, contact your banks and credit companies again. They should be able to inform you if any withdrawals or charges were made by the crooks and how to file a claim. It's imperative that you do all of these things within two or three days.

For a stolen passport, see the following site: studentsabroad.state.gov (Travel Docs > Lost or Stolen Passports). The Social Security fraud line is 1-800-269-0271, or you can file a report on their website at oig.ssa.gov/report.

Numbers of the three national credit bureaus are: EQUIFAX (800-685-1111), TRANSUNION (800-888-4213), EXPERIAN (888-397-3742).

42. STDs, HIV, AIDS

No war on the face of the Earth is more destructive than the AIDS pandemic.
— Colin Powell

STDs, HIV, and AIDS are ubiquitous. Many of them are viral and incurable. They are contracted in various ways: sexual contact, exchange of bodily fluid, sharing syringes, or having a blood transfusion.

You can greatly reduce the risks by using a condom, but a condom isn't foolproof, and prior medical testing of your partner is no guarantee of present or future disease. Even in a monogamous relationship, you can never be sure. Some students acquire these diseases while they are studying abroad; others are infected before they go.

It is hard to comprehend these diseases until you meet people who have them. An estimated 32.2 to 37.2 million people are living with HIV or AIDS and 1.5 million people die from it every year.[9] I have friends who contracted HIV and other STDs in the same locations and programs that I've been. It's eye opening.

---

[9] UNAIDS 2014 Global Fact Sheet, http://www.unaids.org.

43. Harassment

Of the delights of this world, man cares most for sexual intercourse. He will go to any length for it—risk fortune, character, reputation, life itself. — Mark Twain

In some parts of the world, women are socialized to view sexual harassment as normal behavior of men. They see harassment as harmless, unless it escalates to unconsenting sex, and that's another complex issue.

No matter who you are or where you come from, you have a right and responsibility to patrol your surroundings and protect yourself. When the wrong person gets too close, your body triggers an internal alarm. It's up to you to listen and respond correctly. You wouldn't hide under your bed if a fire alarm went off in your house and you wouldn't run outside in the event of a tornado.

Rape isn't about sex; it's about power. Men who rape are ravaging wolves that carefully select their prey and wait for an opportunity to strike. They don't want to get hurt in the process, so they choose those who they think are naïve, weak, and won't put up a fight. They don't want to get caught, so they wait for the right opportunity.

When out, portray yourself as confident, with boundaries. Be assertive not only with words, but with your body language and behaviors, too. Even if you look vulnerable to an attacker, you can take away his opportunity with vigilance.

Beware of the colorless, tasteless, and odorless date-rape drugs like Rohypnol. These drugs depress the central nervous system. Rapists slip them into your drink and within a half hour, they begin to take effect. Victims are unable to refuse sex due to physical helplessness and can't remember what happened. If you think you've been drugged, get to a safe place immediately, ask for help from a trusted friend, and file a police report.

44. The legal system

Liberty is the right of doing whatever the laws permit.
— Charles Montesquieu

As a U.S. citizen in a foreign country, you are subject to the laws of that country. One of the biggest legal problems that students face abroad is drugs. Other problems are alcohol and disorderly behavior. More than 2,000 Americans are arrested every year, and half of the arrests are on drug-related charges. There is very little that the U.S. government can do if you're arrested in a foreign country. No magic wands, no special deals, no signing on the dotted line and you're out.

The system and penalties may not offer the same or similar protections at they do in the United States. If you're arrested, you can expect a visit from a U.S. consular officer who can notify your family or friends, give you a list of attorneys, and help you obtain legal representation. You can also expect the officer to intercede with local authorities to help assure your rights under the country's legal system, by protesting abuse to the authorities in line with internationally accepted standards. The officer cannot demand your release, represent you in a trial, give you legal advice, or pay your legal fees.

You don't have to do something really bad to break the law and go to jail. Students have been arrested for carrying medications that are considered illegal narcotics; for inadvertently trying to make a purchase on a credit card that will exceed the limit; for taking photographs of a government, police, or military building; for purchasing or trying to leave the country with souvenirs that customs authorities believe are national treasures; for carrying a package for someone, which unknowingly contains illegal drugs; for participating in demonstrations or strikes, and more. Don't make assumptions about the law; learn the law and how to be safe.

45. Embassies and consulates

An ambassador is an honest man sent abroad to lie for his country.
— Henry Wotton, Sr.

Both embassies and consulates represent their governments and are exclusively located in foreign countries. Embassies speak for their national governments in foreign countries, and consulates provide diplomatic services to individuals and businesses, such as visas and trade, but both work together in various ways. They provide emergency and non-emergency assistance for all kinds of situations. They also provide safety, security, and other useful information.

Embassies are always located in the capital city (the seat of foreign government), and consulates are located in one or more other major cities with a large population. In Ecuador, the U.S. embassy is located in Quito, while the consulate is in Guayaquil. Depending on the nature of your inquiry, you may be directed to one or the other. In some countries, there is a consular section of the embassy in the capital city. In other countries, there is a consulate but no embassy, usually to preserve diplomatic relations with a third country.

When there's an emergency affecting U.S. citizens, the Embassy will usually broadcast information via their web site, email lists, phone trees, warden network, and local media channels. If the disaster is of a large-enough scale and if the situation warrants it, the Embassy may advise all Americans to evacuate the country, and may even provide the means to do so, with the assistance of the U.S. Department of State and the U.S. Military. It is the responsibility of U.S. citizens to take an active role in this process.

The Embassy's evacuation plan has one objective: to help you move away from an area of possible danger as safely and quickly as possible. In some countries, you must get yourself to the closest Evacuation Control Center. When planning for possible emergencies, go to your embassy's website, and look up their evacuation procedures. If there are Evacuation Control Centers, map it out. Bring your passport, birth certificate, or other primary evidence of U.S. citizenship.

Emergency	General	No Service
Some assistance for serious legal, medical, and financial trouble. Evacuation in case of a disaster.	Absentee voting, visas, permits, tax forms, notarizing documents, local information , etc.	Tourism, missing luggage, obtaining foreign documents, translations, legal advice and service.

WEBSITES
Register with the State Department: step.state.gov
U.S. Embassies & Consulates: usembassy.gov
OSAC (Security Advisory Council): osac.gov

FINANCIALS ABROAD

46. Bringing money

Yesterday is a canceled check; tomorrow is a promissory note; today is the only cash you have – so spend it wisely. — Kay Lyon

Bring some cash for emergency. Exchange it at the airport, or outside of the airport for a better rate. For most of your visit, though, plan to either open a bank account or use ATMs (CIRRUS and PLUS are popular and accessible) to withdraw cash from your bank at home. ATMs usually offer the most favorable exchange rates.

If you plan to use your ATM card in conjunction with your bank at home, check that your pin is valid, and verify the amount of service charge invoked for each transaction. Also, check to make your ATM card is working and will not expire while you're abroad. Have a backup plan in case your ATM card stops working, or gets damaged, lost, or stolen. Credit cards are accepted widely, and usually also have favorable exchange rates when making purchases.

Find out which credit cards are most popular in the countries where you will be traveling. Discover Card, for example, is accepted only on a limited basis outside of the Americas. American Express, MasterCard, and Visa are most prevalent, and are therefore, your safest bets. Look into transaction fees before you commit to a credit card. Different banks can charge anywhere from zero to three percent.

If you are thinking about opening a bank account, then think also about the exchange rates and whether or not it might be to your advantage or disadvantage to deposit a large amount of money when you arrive. Obviously, if the U.S. dollar is getting weaker, and it's certainly a possibility, then you'd want to invest in the foreign currency as soon as possible. If it's getting stronger, then it might serve you better to withdraw cash from home, on an as-needed basis.

If you're planning to withdraw large sums of cash to pay rent, then consider getting a local bankcard or opening an online banking account. Rather than paying ATM fees to withdraw your money from home, you'll pay a small fee for each transfer. Try to limit your transfers in order to better monitor your cash flow and save. Use the Automated Clearinghouse (ACH) system if you can wait two or three days; this is cheaper than same-day wires.

47. Saving money

A penny saved is a dollar earned. — Benjamin Franklin

One of the best ways to save money is with grants and scholarships, if you take time to apply. My college roommate wanted to study abroad, but her parents wouldn't help her with the cost. Because she was so determined, she applied for every grant and scholarship she could find. She ended up with two big awards, studied abroad for a semester in Italy, and came back home with more money than she had before she left.

Saving money is both religious and creative. It's religious in the sense that it involves organizing priorities, exercising self-discipline, and making sacrifices. It's creative because you have to get the next best alternative, for less. You won't be able to save if you don't believe that every little bit counts. I know people who bring in twice as much income as others, but live at the same standard or lower.

TIPS FOR SAVING MONEY ABROAD

Always research and compare to find the best value.

Understand the local currency and familiarize yourself with coins and bills, so you don't overpay.

Know the prices for different items you commonly buy and know where to buy them for less.

Look for special student rates and discounts. Consider buying an International Student ID Card.

Shop where the locals shop. Outdoor markets usually offer the freshest produce, and they're fun.

Use debit cards at ATMs for favorable exchange rates.

Buy your guidebooks in the United States before you leave.

Look at the different ways in which you can use public transportation (day passes, weekly passes, monthly passes, student passes).

Bring your lunch to school, if it costs less than it would to buy something at the cafeteria.

Buy train tickets and rail passes ahead of time; this requires pre-planning.

Take overnight trains en lieu of paying for hotels.

Consider hostels en lieu of hotels or motels.

Eat in outdoor markets, grocery stores, or small cafes as opposed to expensive, fancy restaurants.

Check menu prices before you decide on a restaurant.

Know the tipping customs. In many parts of the world, tips are already in the bill.

Buy generic instead of name brand products, if you're not sacrificing too much quality.

Don't be afraid to buy second-hand and used items.

48. Exchanging money

Money is like a sixth sense – and you can't make use of the other five without it.
— William Somerset Maugham

Don't exchange money in hotels, restaurants, or shops if you want the best rates. Don't exchange money on the street because it's illegal, but also because of many scams. In some countries, crooks give you worthless currency from another nation that looks like the currency you need, or they give you counterfeit bills. By the time you figure it out, they're gone.

Official exchange booths at international airports or in town are the best way to change cash. You can also change it in banks. ATMs usually offer the best rates and are hassle-free for withdrawing money. Be sure to have some cash and a credit card on hand if your ATM cards are lost, stolen, or eaten by the machines.

Paying with a credit card is an option, too. Visa, MasterCard, and American Express offer competitive exchange rates and are commonly accepted in Europe, Latin America, and Asia. For the sake of convenience, I use a credit card as much as possible, and pay it off every month to avoid interest. Be sure to know your pins. While you wouldn't want to make a habit of drawing cash on credit, you may need to do so in case of an emergency.

49. Working abroad

The world is full of willing people, some willing to work, the rest willing to let them. — Robert Frost

Whether or not you can work really depends on the flexibility of your visa. Check with the consulate that issued your visa for restrictions. Then check with the host institution about part-time jobs. Don't study abroad unless you know that you can pay for it, since there are no guarantees for employment. It may be better to get a loan, even if you don't use it.

There are advantages and disadvantages to working while you study abroad. Working can give you some extra cash and help you get to know the locals, but it takes time away from your studies and travel. Coursework abroad can be more difficult than in the United States so you may need extra time just to keep up in class. Only you can gauge what's best, based on what you hope to get out of the experience.

If you're not allowed to work in the host country, there are other ways to earn money without getting a job. I know of one student who decided to play music on the street for loose change and donations; unbelievably, he ended up bringing in a lot of extra cash. Other students babysit, teach English, or do odd jobs for locals that need help.

Teaching English can be fun, but it isn't easy. It takes a great deal of time and patience to teach languages. Contact U.S. companies that might need help and can benefit from your location abroad. Maybe a travel publisher or website would be willing to pay you to try out different hotels, cafes, etc. and write up a section in their upcoming book or on their blog.

Another option for work is through the Internet. Do you have some marketable skill? If so, become a freelancer. You can do the work from wherever you are and have the payments deposited into your checking account at home, which you can then withdraw using an ATM. There are a variety of online companies that connect businesses with freelancers.

50. Running out of money

Beware of little expenses; a small leak will sink a great ship. — Benjamin Franklin

If you run out of money, ask someone back home for help. There are many ways to get money into your hands. The free and easy way is to have it deposited into your checking account from home, so you can withdraw it overseas at an ATM. If this is not an option for you, then you can have someone wire or send it through a service.

American Express money orders can be initiated in the United States and completed at an office branch abroad. Other options include PayPal, Dwolla (U.S. bank accounts only), Transferwise, or similar services like Neteller and Moneybookers. Western Union tends to be fairly reasonable and convenient for many people.

51. Paying taxes

The hardest thing in the world to understand is the income tax. — Albert Einstein

There are many different taxes in other countries. Value Added Tax (VAT) is a regressive tax in the EU on the added value that results from exchanges. It is different from sales tax, which is levied on the total value. As a visitor who resides outside of the EU, you can get a refund on purchases you take home. Look for stores with a "Tax-Free Shopping" logo in the window. When purchasing something for export, just present your non-EU passport and ask for a Global Refund Check. When you exit the country, the check should be stamped by customs officials and taken to a Global Refund Office in the airport for cash, check, direct credit, or bank deposit.

Watch out for scams with the VAT. Some stores tell you that you can get a refund at the airport, but your purchase receipt reads that you have already received the refund directly from the shop, and worse of all, you signed the receipt, stating that you received it! One thing you can do to avoid this scam and others is not to sign what you have not read or have not completely understood in the foreign language. The only thing you should be signing is a credit card slip that authorizes payment. If you don't read the language, and the clerk insists that you sign, then kindly ask someone to translate the document.

Don't forget to file your income tax return or an extension if you need more time. As a U.S. student residing abroad, you are still obligated to pay income tax under U.S. tax laws and must file a state and federal return if your gross income is over a certain amount. Gross income is all your earnings in any given tax year (wages, overseas income, self-employment income, interest, dividends, etc.). It may also include scholarships. Pell Grants, Supplemental Educational Opportunity Grants, and Grants to States for State Student Exceptions are nontaxable scholarships to the extent used for tuition and course-related expenses during the grant period. If your host employer takes out income taxes, then you may be eligible for a deduction or refund. Check with the IRS.

The U.S. now has income tax treaties with more than 35 other countries, which means that international taxing authorities can exchange financial information. So, do not fudge on your tax return. Even interest you have earned through a foreign bank account is taxable. If you have bank accounts in another country with more than $10,000, then you must file annually FBAR, Report of Foreign Bank and Financial Accounts. Publication 54, *The Tax Guide for U.S. Citizens Abroad* will answer your questions.

52. Traveling cheap

Frugality may be termed the daughter of Prudence, the sister of Temperance, and the parent of Liberty — Samuel Johnson

If you plan carefully, you shouldn't need a lot of money to travel around. A little cash can go a long way abroad.

Choose hostels instead of motels and hotels. While there are different types of hostels, typically you provide your own towels and sleep sack (a sheet folded and hemmed). Bedrooms and bathrooms are often shared by guests; however, single rooms may be available for a higher price. You will probably have self-serve kitchen facilities.

Hostelling is a culture unto itself for those who are adventurous, independent, and frugal. While people from all walks of life use hostels, they are especially popular among backpackers and those who are traveling for long periods of time (ex. a twelve-week trip around Australia and New Zealand). Hosteling is an excellent way to see and do more, meet people from everywhere, and learn about the culture and country. An alternative to staying in hostels is to stay with people you know in other areas of the world. If you have a desire to stay in people's homes, consider SERVAS International at servas.org.

KNOW BEFORE YOU GO

53. Time is an investment

When we are doing what we love, we don't care about time. For at least at that moment, time doesn't exist and we are truly free. — Marcia Wieder

You'll make a lot of choices about your time while you study abroad. Some students will travel throughout their study abroad experience, to see as many places as possible. Others will stay put and really get to know the people and places in their area. There is nothing wrong with either investment, if it's going to enhance your education and satisfies your goals.

If fostering friendships with locals is important to you, be careful about how much time you spend with other Americans. When you're with Americans all the time, you run the risk of dissociating yourself from the local community. Be mindful that all individuals lead to groups, and a relationship with one local can lead to many more.

54. Misunderstandings happen

The most beautiful discovery true friends make is that they can grow separately without growing apart. — Elisabeth Foley

No matter whom you are socializing with, some miscommunications will occur. It's all part of the experience. Maybe you're studying in Mexico, and you think it'd be nice to invite your host mother out to dinner one night, since she's always cooking for you. When it's time to leave, the whole family and extended family show up, and after dinner, the bill is handed to you. What you just learned about Mexican culture is an invitation to some family members is an open invitation to all, and the person who extended the initial invitation is the one responsible for the bill. Ouch!

If something doesn't go as planned, and it costs you time, money, or pride, do your best to fix the situation, and learn from the experience. It's over, so don't dwell on it. Make a concerted effort to be humble, considerate, and respectful of the culture. Help with chores. Ask permission to take items from the refrigerator or to use the phone. Don't use too much water or electricity, as it's very expensive in other countries. If your family doesn't wear shoes in the house, then you shouldn't either. Listen and observe. Never forget that you're a guest.

55. Student life

Travel and change of place impart new vigor to the mind. — Seneca

First, university life is different in other countries. The institution may not have a campus, but rather buildings spread around the city. Students may be older than twenty-two and may live at home, eliminating the need for on-campus residence halls and university-sponsored clubs and activities. The Student Union may be completely independent. Young people may play sports or engage in other activities for fun. Students may spend more time with their families than they do with friends. Their best friends may be family members: brothers, sisters, and cousins.

In many countries, professors give lectures and assign readings but students are responsible for how much work they do and what they really accomplish. Most learning requires self-discipline and direction. Rather than being evaluated on class participation, pop quizzes, and tests, students are graded on one or two final examinations. This can be nerve-racking, but is a good indication of whether or not you've retained the information taught in the course. The relationship between a professor and students is usually more formal than in the United States, and there may be no explanation provided for assigned grades.

The system may be different as well. In the United States, registration is usually a painless online process, a class meets in the same room for the entire quarter or semester, you receive a syllabus of some kind at the beginning of a course, and organization is apparent. In foreign countries, registration may be a painful paper-driven process, your classrooms may switch location frequently, you may not be provided with a syllabus, and organization is not always apparent. Also, students may follow a rigid plan of study with little to no say in their schedules. The same course may change substantially from one professor to another.

Libraries may not be the self-serve setup that you're used to at home and access to materials may be limited. Usually, you have to request materials from a librarian or via a computer. The books are then retrieved, and you can schedule a time to review or pick them up. For security reasons, you may have to check your backpack at a desk upon entering the library and the library may not be open late at night. It takes a while to get used to the schedule and procedures. Always allow extra time when learning new systems. If you're attending an American university overseas, then this information may be irrelevant.

What is often considered normal practice in foreign countries may appear disorganized and backwards to Americans. Student Services is an American concept that may not exist abroad, especially at public institutions. American parents and students pay a lot of money for college and expect good service. In other countries, education is regarded as a privilege rather than a product, because the system is not driven by consumer spending. Consider a book, *Understanding the Education—and through it the Culture—in Education Abroad* by Linda A. Chrisholm and Howard A. Beny.

56. Getting around

It is not down on any map; true places never are. — Herman Melville

Most students use public transportation while they are living abroad. In fact, public transportation is generally the preferred method of getting around. Not many countries are afforded the kind of space and resources that we have in the United States. It is easier just to hop on a metro, bus, or train, than it is to drive and search for parking.

For short trips, walking is great, or you can buy a used bicycle and ride it for your entire stay. In general, you'll find that people walk and bike a lot more in other countries than they do in the United States, just to get around. It's refreshing to see even old ladies and gentlemen out and about.

If you're in Europe or the U.K., the best way to travel to other cities and countries is via trains and planes. Believe it or not, it can sometimes be cheaper to take a plane than a train. Many years ago, I paid €12 to fly from one European country to another on a budget airline. Beware, baggage weight limits may be low, and excess fees may be high. So, if you don't plan carefully, it can cost a lot more in the end.

Eurail (eurail.com) and Eurostar (eurostar.com) are some of the best rails to get around. Eurail is for travel around Europe, and Eurostar is for travel within the U.K. See raileurope.com for the major providers of rail passes. While not as swift as flying, you get to see the countryside and the journey is more enjoyable. Visit Rick Steves to download the latest rail guide: ricksteves.com/rail.

BUDGET AIRLINES
Easyjet – easyjet.com
Icelandair – icelandair.is
Ryanair – ryanair.com
Wizzair – wizzair.com

TRAINS
France – sncf.com
Germany – reiseauskunft.bahn.de
Italy– trenitalia.it
Spain – renfe.es/ingles
U.K. – nationalrail.co.uk

TAXI TIPS
Don't use unregistered (independent) taxis. Learn how to identify an authentic cab in your host country.

Find taxi stands where only authorized taxis are allowed to stop and pick up passengers. Know how many passengers are permitted.

Look for similarities among taxis, phone numbers, identification numbers, meters, radios, etc.

Know what different rides cost in the city, and make sure you have enough cash to cover the cost.

Make sure there is a meter running or negotiate a price, before you get into the car, to avoid rip-offs.

Know the general route to where you are going, so that you can confront a taxi that takes you for a ride.

Be careful about sharing taxis with strangers, because scams are often attempted by pairs and groups.

Avoid taxis in front of train stations and airports to dodge high prices and rip-offs.

Make sure there's an inside handle. Also, make sure it works and you can get out of the car if it becomes necessary.

Keep an eye on your bags. Leave your bag in the event of an emergency.

Know who to call when you have an emergency (your local 911).

DRIVING

Some students choose to buy a car when they travel overseas. Usually a group of friends will pitch in to buy something old and cheap, but it's not advisable. You don't know the condition of the car, and it could be unsafe. You also need an international driver's license, registration paperwork, license plates, insurance, operation, maintenance, repairs, and much more. The laws are different in other countries and in case of an accident, there may be a whole lot of trouble that you didn't see coming. The driving culture can also be complicated, especially for a foreigner. Many students die in vehicles that other students are driving.

Go to routesinternational.com for world transportation by road, rail, sea, and air. You can find links to local buses, subways, and ferries.

Go to youra.com/intlferries/index.html to link to ferry operations around the world.

For over 2000 walks in the UK and Europe, visit walkingworld.com.

57. Measurements

Any measurement must take into account the position of the observer. There is no such thing as measurement absolute, there is only measurement relative. — Jeanette Winterson

The metric system is a decimal-based system of measurement, introduced by France in 1799. It was originally based on the meter and kilogram. The imperial system was introduced in the United Kingdom and its colonies, including Commonwealth countries. It uses ounces and pounds for weight, fluid ounces and gallons for volume, and inches and feet for length. There is also the International Systems of Units (SI), the most widely used system of measurement. In this system, a space is used to separate hundreds, and it doesn't distinguish between the comma and the period in decimals. For example, $15 500,50 is the same as $15 500.50. In the United States, the comma is often used to separate thousands ($1,000) and the period is used for decimals ($10.95). However, in Continental Europe, it is just the opposite; the period is used to separate thousands ($1.000) and the comma is used for decimals ($10,95).

GENERAL

Length	Area
1 inch = 2.54 centimeters	1 square mile = 2.59 sq km
1 centimeter = .39 inches	1 square kilometer = .386 sq mi
1 foot = .30 meters	1 sq miles = 259 hectares
1 meter = 3.281 feet	1 hectare = 100 acres
1 yard = .9144 meters	1 sq kilometer = 247.1 acres
1 mile = 1.61 kilometers	100 acres = .01 sq kilometer

STUDY ABROAD MAP

1 kilometer = .62 miles	Kilometers (km), miles (mi), square (sq)
Volume	*Weight*
1 gallon = 3.785 liters	1 pound = .45 kilograms
1 liter = .264 gallons	1 kilogram = 2.2 pounds
1 fl ounce = 29.6 milliliters	1 ounce = 28.3 grams
1 milliliters = .03 fl ounces	1 gram = .04 ounces
1 cup = 8 ounces	1 cup = 100 grams dry weight
Speed	Energy & Temperature
1 mph = 1.609 kmh	1 hp = 0.7457 kW
1 kmh = .62 mph	1 kW = 1.341hp
1 kn = 1.85 kmh	1 cal = 4.2 J
1 kmh = .54 kn	1 J = .24 cal
	$C = (F - 32)/1.8$
	$F = (C \times 1.8) + 32$
Kilometers per hour (kmh), miles per hour (mph), international knots (kn)	Horse power (hp), kilowatts (kW), calories (cal), joules (J), Fahrenheit (F), Celsius (C)

TEMPERATURE

There are two main temperature scales: Fahrenheit (used in the United States) and Celsius (part of the Metric System, used in most countries). Daniel Gabriel Fahrenheit (1686-1736) proposed his system first in 1724, whereas Anders Celsius (1701-1744) proposed his system in 1742, just two years before his death. Notice that Fahrenheit is 180 degrees between the freezing and boiling points of water and Celsius is only 100. You can easily make conversions between the two.

°C to °F   Multiply by 9, Divide by 5, Add 32

°F to °C   Subtract 32, Multiply by 5, Divide by 9

	Celsius	Fahrenheit
Freezing point of water	0 °C	32 °F
Ideal weather	21 °C	70 °F
Body Temperature	37 °C	98.6 °F
Hot bath water	40 °C	104 °F
Boiling point of water	100 °C	212 °F

CLOTHING (PANTS)

Women

U.S.	2	4	6	8	10	12	14	16
Australia	6	8	10	12	14	16	18	20
U.K.	4	6	8	10	12	14	16	18
Italy	36	38	40	42	44	46	48	50
France	32	34	36	38	40	42	44	46
Germany	30	32	34	36	38	40	42	44
Japan	5	7	9	11	13	15	17	19

Men

U.S.	32	34	36	38	40	42	44	46
U.K.	32	34	36	38	40	42	44	46
Cont Eur	42	44	46	48	50	52	54	56

Japan		S		M	L		LL	

CLOTHING (SHOES)

Women

U.S.	6	6.5	7	7.5	8	8.5	9	9.5
Australia	4.5	5	5.5	6	6.5	7	7.5	8
U.K.	3.5	4	4.5	5	5.5	6	6.5	7
Con Eur	36	37	37.5	38	38.5	39	40	41
Korea	235	238	241	245	248	251	254	257
Japan	22	22.5	23	23.5	24	24.5	25	25.5

Men

U.S.	6	6.5	7	7.5	8	8.5	9	9.5
U.K.	5.5	6	6.5	7	7.5	8	8.5	9

Cont Eur	38	38.5	39	40	41	42	43	43.5
Japan	24	24.5	25	25.5	26	26.5	27	27.5

ELECTRICITY

U.S. current = 110 volts, 60 cycles of alternating current. Most other countries are between 220 to 240 volts.

58. Food and drink

The belly rules the mind. — Spanish Proverb

Eating is the highlight of all my travels, both national and international. I love good food. In Italy, I discovered the slow-food movement founded by Carlo Petrini. It promotes local natural food and traditional cooked, contrary to fast food. Try as many ethnic foods as you can. While you will likely have the opportunity to eat special and exotic dishes, it probably won't be every day. I ate snake and monkey once, and guinea pig twice in the Peace Corps. Many foods are the same we eat in the United States, but they are grown and prepared differently. A country's food is the hand of her hospitality. If you don't eat her food, you don't fully accept her hospitality.

Avoid getting sick by having hard fast rules about your food. In areas where water is not potable, consume boiled and bottled water, carbonated beverages, beer, and wine. Avoid unpasteurized milk products, and only eat raw fruit or vegetables that are washed in treated water and peeled. As the saying goes, "Cook it, boil it, peel it, or forget it." Remember, people can get brain worms from eating healthy foods like berries that are contaminated with fecal matter.

59. Bathrooms

If I want to be alone, some place I can write, I can read, I can pray, I can cry, I can do whatever I want – I go to the bathroom. — Alicia Keys

Bathrooms in other countries can be amusing, simply because they are different from what you may be accustomed to in the United States. Handles and buttons to flush the toilet may be extra-large or extra-small. Bathtubs and showers may have strange mechanisms. In some developing nations, for example, it is common to see a Frankenstein lever that you push up to turn on the electricity and make your shower run hot. If you touch any of the metal in the shower while the lever is up, you get an electrical shock.

Bathrooms may also have different unspoken rules. In developing nations, the sewer system usually isn't equipped to handle toilet paper, so people put it in the trashcan rather than flush it down the bowl. There may be no push button or lever to flush the toilet; instead, you throw a bucket of water in the bowl. Alternatively, there may be no toilets at all, just holes; no bathtubs and showers, only a bucket. People may not use toilet paper; instead, a teapot full of water and their left hand, which is actually a cleaner way to go. Or, water may burst up from the toilet and clean you automatically, sort-of like a car wash.

In the public arena, there may not be a separate bathroom for women and men, and you may have to pay some money to use it. Typically, public facilities don't provide amenities like toilet paper and soap, so keep a stash in your purse or daypack. It is not uncommon for people to sell toilet paper at the entrance either. Don't eat any sketchy foods while on the road or before a long trip. It's no fun to get sick on a bus full of strangers.

For a good laugh, see <u>toilet-guru.com</u> (Toilets of the World).

60. Laundry

After enlightenment, the laundry. — Zen Proverb

Every country is different when it comes to how people do laundry. If going to Western Europe, you'll probably be using machines, but in some parts of the world, be prepared to learn how to wash your clothes the old-fashioned way. While there are usually washers, there are not always dryers. If dryers aren't common, bring a clothesline or buy one upon arrival.

If you have to wash your clothes by hand, there are washboards or platforms that assist in the process and water flows directly into them. In some countries, you may have to wash your clothes and take a bath using a bucket. Actually, your clothes come out cleaner after hand washing them than throwing them in a machine; so don't fret over it. Ask for assistance if you can't figure it out.

If you dry your clothing on a line outside, be careful about when and for how long. In parts of Africa, flies can leave their diseased eggs on your wet clothing. You can also get body lice and crabs if you dry your underwear on couches, chairs, or beds where people put their heads. If you are on or near the equator, beware of the sun, which can burn white clothing and turn it yellow or light brown.

Tip—on the road, wash out your lighter clothing (underwear and socks) the night before and they should be dry in the morning. If it's cold, try putting them near the radiator or heat vent. If you are staying in the same place for more than two nights, then wash larger items in the bathtub or shower, as long as they have two or three days to dry. There's no need for detergent because bar soap works fine.

61. Cell phones and Internet

If it keeps up, man will atrophy all his limbs but the push-button finger. — Frank Lloyd Wright

A cell phone is handy, but don't bring one with you unless it is unlocked and uses GSM (Global System for Mobile Communications) standard, the most popular mobile phone system in the world. With an unlocked GSM phone, you can buy a SIM and get a local number. Buying a pre-paid SIM overseas is usually much cheaper and easier than using an international plan or roaming with a company at home. You receive calls for free, unlike the United States where you have to pay to place or receive calls. Alternatively, you can buy a phone in your host country and pay as you go.

It really depends on your location, but most likely you will have access to the Internet either at school or in your apartment. Don't expect Internet access to be as prevalent or as fast as it is at home. In the United States, many families have several computers as well as cable or DSL Internet access in their homes. For economic and cultural reasons, this isn't always the case in other parts of the world.

If you have Internet, there are lots of messaging apps that allow you to call people for free all over the world. You'll need to figure out how the local phone system works and how to place in-country and international calls. Here are some examples:

PLACING A CALL TO ITALY FROM NORTH AMERICA
Phone: +39 06 466229
Fax: +39 06 46622900 (fax numbers may be longer than phone numbers in European countries)

The + reminds you to add your international access code, which is 011 if dialing from North America. "39" is the Country Code for Italy. "06" is the Area Code for Rome. Dial 011 (access), 39 (country code), 06 (city code), 466229 (local number).

PLACING A CALL TO NORTH AMERICA FROM ITALY
Phone: (217) 556-5678

To call North America, just dial 001 (the 00 is the direct dial prefix, and the 1 is the country code) and then 217-556-5678.

PLACING A CALL TO GERMANY FROM ITALY
You see the phone number written two different ways:

+49 69 7578-1130 and 069 7578-1130

The first way assumes you're calling from another country. The + reminds you to add your international access code, which is 00 if dialing from anywhere in Europe (except Finland).

The second way assumes you're calling from Germany. Since Germany uses an area code, drop the first "0" when calling from another country.

Dial 00 (access), 49 (country code), 69 (area code), and 7578-1130 (local number).

PLACING A CALL WITHIN YOUR HOST COUNTRY
Some countries use area codes and others use direct-dial. For those that use area codes, you have to dial the area code first. For those that use direct-dial, you just dial the same number no matter where it is in the country. There may still be long-distance charges, so check before you dial.

62. Snail mail

What a lot we lost when we stopped writing letters. You can't reread a phone call. — Liz Carpenter

The postal service can be very different in other countries. In the United States, you are probably accustomed to a postal worker dropping off mail, in a box outside of your home, on a daily basis. You are likely inundated with junk mail and bills, along with a few personal letters here and there.

Fortunately, many countries don't use the postal service as much as we do or in the same way. For example, in Ecuador, I had to physically go to a building to pay my water and electric bill. In Italy, we didn't get junk mail like we did in the United States.

Thanks to email, you probably won't have to send as many letters via post. However, you may wish to receive packages. In many countries, duty is imposed when you pick up your packages. The amount depends on weight, content, and value. Learn more about this before asking people to send things. Certain items are prohibited for political and health-related reasons. Also, international shipping is usually not insurable through the United States Postal Service (USPS). On the USPS website, you can find a wealth of information about country prohibitions, restrictions, observations, size limitations, customs, and more. Go to pe.usps.gov and select the International Mail Manual.

Keep in mind that foreign postal systems may take longer. I sent a large package to Ecuador via airmail, and it wasn't received until three months later. It is not uncommon for letters and packages to take several weeks or months for delivery. Always write "air mail" on your international package, as it can still go by boat if you don't.

Avoid sending perishable or irreplaceable valuables or money in the mail. If sending more than $50 worth of stuff, it is best to ascertain that the contents are insured for theft, loss, and damage, by sending through a provider like UPS or DHL. You will probably have to pay some sort of duty. As a rule of thumb, if you can get it where you are, even if it costs a little more, it's probably better to buy it locally. The cost of shipping is horrendous.

When I was living abroad, a friend of mine sent me a care package full of used clothing and snacks. On the customs form, she wrote $100 as the value of the contents. Consequently, it cost me about $20 in duty fees (20% of the value) to get it out of customs. Lesson learned: if the value of the package is relative, then estimate low (ex. used clothing could be worthless). If your sender writes zero then most packages should be free to pick up.

On another note, when I lived in Africa, my mother sent me a pair of shoes. Anyway, she was very clever; she sent each shoe in a different package. After all, who would try to steal just one? I ended up receiving the second one a month later, but I can't complain because it arrived! If she hadn't done that, I'm sure my shoes would have been conveniently lost or stolen in the mail. The black markets love good stuff made in the United States

If you don't have an address right away, no worries. Most of the time, you can have mail sent in care of the international programs office until you find a place to live. In some countries, there are no mail carriers or addresses, so you have to get a post office box to receive mail.

63. Markets and bargaining

Don't bargain for fish which are still in the water. — Indian Proverb

Bargaining is a social and business practice in most countries. By virtue of the fact that you're a tourist, you will have to learn to bargain if you want a fair price. If you're not accustomed to bargaining, you may feel uneasy at first. Stick with it and learn from your mistakes. It's actually pleasant and fun once you get the hang of it.

Know where to shop and when. Tourist markets are expensive. Unless you want to buy gifts and souvenirs for your trip home, then you'll probably want to shop where the locals shop. Any local can tell you where to go, just ask. All the locals know where to get clothes, produce, and miscellaneous things for a fair price.

Know the market value for whatever it is that you want to buy. You can ask the locals (friends), or you can check in a few stores to see what kind of price they give you. People like to help. Don't stand in stiff, proud, cultural shoes and pretend to know everything. Let people assist, but not the same people who you are negotiating with, please.

Decide what you want to buy and the most that you're willing to pay relative to its fair market value. Then, look at several different items without letting on to the one you really like. Ask for prices. Pick an item that you want, and then start negotiating below the price or below what you're willing to pay, whichever is less. Don't let the salesperson see your enthusiasm for the item. Make it look as if you're kind-of interested but not sold because there are other options you can consider elsewhere.

There's no rule about where you should start negotiating. If you know the fair market value, then you should start below it, so that you can arrive at something fair. If you don't know the fair market value, then you should know how much vendors typically mark up their prices, which may vary by city, market, and store.

I usually subtract sixty percent in hopes of arriving at fifty percent off the price, or I start below what I am willing to pay and go higher. If they don't agree with my highest price, then I thank them kindly, and walk away. If the salesperson is willing to take my price, but was bluffing to see if he could get more, then he'll call me back or send his son or daughter to call me back.

Be careful not to go too low when you start negotiating or the salesperson will either be insulted or will assume that you don't have a clue about the market or how much to pay for things. He'll probably start trying to teach you about market prices, while making it look as if he's giving you a deal.

If you're having a tough time getting a lower price, look for a reason it should be reduced like a flaw or defect. Tell the sales person that he is going to have a hard time finding a buyer for an imperfect product that needs fixing or work.

If you're buying several items, ask for a discount, and if they won't give you a discount, then ask for a free item or gift. If they won't give you a gift, then just forget it. What's important is you got what you wanted at a price you were willing to pay.

Don't buy antiques! Antiques are often considered national treasures and are illegal to take out of the country. People are arrested at airports every year for innocently trying to export antique coins, paintings, sculptures, etc.

Always take your purchase with you; don't have it shipped home. If you have to ship it, make sure that it's covered by insurance or secure, money-back guarantees if damaged, lost, stolen in the mail, or never mailed at all.

64. Hosting guests

We are all visitors to this time, this place. We are just passing through. Our purpose here is to observe, to learn, to grow, to love...and then we return home. — Australian Aboriginal Proverb

Know the rules of your housing complex before inviting anyone to stay with you. It is common for residence halls to have restrictions regarding guests, and you shouldn't expect your host family to provide space either. When my parents visited me, they stayed at a family-run hostel that operated like a bed and breakfast. It was more pleasant for them than staying in my cramped quarters. It also gave them some necessary down time.

Some universities have their own housing, available for free or much less than market prices. If not, they will usually have discounts with local hotels. Some universities also have visiting parent programs, where the institution provides them with a wealth of information, tips, discounts, a tour of the campus, and complementary meals. If there is nothing like this at your host institution, then check to see if the visitor's office can arrange for a tour.

It is ideal if parents and friends come to visit you during your vacation time or after the program has ended. That way you don't have to worry about your academic workload. Also, you will have been there long enough to show them how to navigate the country and culture. It's no fun trying to entertain guests when you're in the middle of final exams or when you are juggling three to five demanding classes.

One thing that you may not have thought about is insurance. Your guest's current health insurance coverage may not be adequate for medical assistance and medical emergency evacuation. They may also wish to purchase trip insurance in case they have to cancel for some reason.

CULTURE AND CUSTOMS

65. Cultural differences

As the soil, however rich it may be, cannot be productive without cultivation, so the mind without culture can never produce good fruit. — Seneca

There are many opinions about what is culture, but fundamentally, it's what we share with other people. Shared experience brings people together with a common set of values and beliefs. There are countless cultures in the world and each of us uniquely fits into many that shape and mold our lives.

A native man from a secluded village of South Africa is part of a different set of cultures than a South African woman whose grandparents migrated to the city. Nonetheless, everyone who is South African has experienced the Apartheid in some way, shape, or form, and there are national bonds they share because of it.

Visiting other countries clues you in to all the intricacies and layers of culture. Just because you're from a particular nation doesn't mean you're exactly the same as other people who live there. Everyone thinks, feels, lives, and behaves according to their own history and beliefs, which are not always apparent. This creates a dynamic human civilization with intercultural connections everywhere.

Culture is not static; it is gradually shifting and changing, and it is very complex. The more you study it, the more amazed you will become by its many different forms in so many nooks and crannies. Culture is the filter we use to communicate. It is something we have but we don't know that we have until we stand face-to-face with another. It is what allows us to maintain individual differences and still come together in community.

Culture is directly related to our worldview, which is how we understand life, death, our earth, and the universe. Linear vs. circular time, direct vs. indirect communication, formality vs. informality, and individualism vs. community are some of the major differences in the way we believe, behave, and subsequently communicate. In Africa, my host mother called a spirit doctor to treat her malaria. When he was locating the spirit, she lovingly ordered me to go into the house because she believed white skin was weak and the spirit could easily find its way into my body.

The problem with cultural differences is we often don't recognize them as differences. There's a story about a Peace Corps volunteer who was teaching in Africa about safe sex and how to put on a condom. For demo purposes, she slid a condom on the end of a broomstick and told them if they do this at home, then they won't get pregnant. A few months later, a woman came back and told the volunteer that it didn't work. She put the condom on the broomstick in her home, but still got pregnant. To the African woman, the volunteer's demonstration was literal, one that fit her worldview.

Suppose your professor is late for his two o'clock class. Through your worldview, he is lazy, disorganized, and even inconsiderate. Why? Because you see your education as a consumer; his time was bought and sold to teach you. However, in his culture, it's expected that both the professor and students will be running late after lunch. Food and friendship is more important than arriving on time.

Global competence is the ability to recognize that one's own worldview does not belong to the world. It's the ability to experience life as the other, without judgment. But no matter how much you think you know about someone, you will experience misunderstandings once in a while. These misunderstandings occur when our communication of values and beliefs clash between worldviews. Good observation is critical. *Maximizing Study Abroad: A Student's Guide to Strategies for Language and Culture Learning and Use* is a great guide for navigating these tricky waters. Other books include *Rethinking Worldview: Learning to Think, Live, and Speak in this World* by J. Mark Bertrand; *The Art of Crossing Cultures* by Craig Storti; and *Beyond Culture* by Edward T. Hall.

Don't be afraid to make mistakes. It's the intention that counts. The ultimate goal is to understand each other, and sometimes understanding your own culture is the best way to start. If you're an American, then you may consider yourself different from other Americans, but chances are you have more in common with your co-nationals than you think. Take the following quiz and count the yeses.

HOW AMERICAN ARE YOU?

Is the ideal person independent and self-reliant?

Do you value your independence and career?

Do you believe that church and state should be kept as separate institutions?

Do you believe religion is an individual choice?

Is the first-come-first-serve outlook fair?

Do you believe that all people are created equal?

Do you prefer informal communication?

Is being on time and punctuality important to you?

Do money and possessions measure success?

Are you accustomed to small talk?

Do you have many different friends?

Do you discuss your personal life openly?

Is a preponderance of evidence necessary to prove something to someone?

Are facts more important than hearsay?

Do you avoid same-sex touch?

When someone you don't know well touches you, does it make you feel uncomfortable?

Do you welcome debate and arguments?

Do you prefer that someone is at least an arm's length away from you when talking?

Is it important that someone look you in the eye for you to know that he is listening?

Are you uncomfortable with silence?

Do you point with your index finger?

Are you free to use both hands in the same way?

Do you take a shower every day?

Do you notice stinky smells easily?

Do you expect to be called by your first name?

Is friendship always informal, regardless of age?

Would you ask a child what he wants to be when he grows up or a senior what she wants to do?

Do you believe in working and playing hard?

Do you enjoy, welcome, and value competition?

Do you have your own space and value privacy?

Do children have the right to disagree with parents?

Do you think that education is the key to success?

Do you believe that everybody has the opportunity to succeed in life, regardless of background?

1-11   12-22   23-33

Not Really Sure   American   Very American

66. Unspoken rules

What you do speaks so loud that I cannot hear what you say. — Ralph Waldo Emerson

Before you go abroad, it is important to know the unspoken rules within the customs and culture. Most of the time, we don't think twice about what we're doing, let alone how it might be offensive. If you knew that direct eye contact was aggressive and rude, then you would avoid it. If you had known that putting your feet on a chair would have resulted in someone spitting on your shoes, then you would have kept them on the floor.

Let's say you are in a highly formal culture. You feel like you have known your professor for a while and call him by his first name. For you, it means you are comfortable with him and like him as a person. You notice your professor's character changes. He seems irritated with you and has more rigid expectations. What do you think might be going on? Well, in his culture, calling him by his first name has inadvertently communicated that you do not respect and honor him as one should his professor.

You should also be careful about what you wear. For example, wearing shorts in a church or having your shoulders exposed is considered disrespectful. Wearing flip flops, sweat pants, a t-shirt, and baseball cap is like wearing an orange sign that says, "I'm an American…yippee!"

Table manners are important in many cultures, and how you conduct yourself at meals. In East Asia, you would not finish everything on your plate. In Belgium, you would never put your hands under the table.

Have respect for people, and that means asking them before you take their photograph, especially if you don't know them.

Learn the different gestures. It's important to know the lewd gestures, so that you don't inadvertently swallow your shoe. The *Peace* sign or the *A-Okay* sign may be quite vulgar in some countries. Shaking your head "No" can mean, "Yes, I hear you" in Asia.

Pay attention to your body language. If you're visiting an African authority figure, don't cross your legs in front of him, as this is a sure sign of disrespect. The way we bow or shake hands may speak volumes about our character in Asia and other parts of the world.

In some countries such as China, any kind of public affection is considered to be rude and inappropriate. Be careful about how you greet people and say goodbye when you depart.

In many Latin countries, personal space is smaller than in the United States, and people stand and sit very close to each other. Italians and Spaniards are especially known to use less personal space.

Smiling at a stranger could be seen as weird or inappropriate in the U.K. Making eye contact could be aggressive or rude in many Asian countries. Lack of facial expression doesn't always mean lack of interest, so don't jump to conclusions.

The Culture Matters Workbook was developed by the Peace Corps to help new Volunteers acquire the knowledge and skills to work successfully and respectfully in other cultures. The URL is quite long, so I advise you search the title using your Internet browser. The *World Citizen's Guide* is a good resource, too: worldcitizensguide.org.

67. Adjustment process

The most important trip you may take in life is meeting people halfway. — Henry Boye

Cultural adjustment, or culture shock, is the path of development through international education. It is to international education as puberty is to growing up. There are five stages involved in cultural adjustment. If you are immersed in the host culture for an extended period, you may experience all five stages. But, if you are traveling on a short-term program or an island program where you are not immersed in the host culture, then you may never leave the first stage.

STAGE 1, EUPHORIA
This stage starts before you leave home. You are excited and when you arrive, everything is great! The orientation is splendid, the people are nice, the food is excellent, and there are so many things to see and do. Everything looks charming, better than you imagined and better than home. Life is good. These feelings last a month or two.

STAGE 2, DISTRESS
You come down from the peak and miss the comforts of home. You're finding it hard to communicate with your host family. You may have gotten sick once or twice. You don't like the poor service at the university. Everything is getting old, and fast! People are beginning to look stupid or act selfish and shallow. You are getting tired, regret your decision to study abroad, and want to go home.

STAGE 3, ADJUSTMENT
Different feelings start to surface in your life. One day you feel embarrassed, and another day you feel isolated, angry, and even hostile. Some days you're happy with your experience and other days you feel depressed. Your experience is not what you expected, but you convince yourself that it's normal and okay. Instead of seeing what is right and wrong with Americans and with the culture you're visiting, you try to understand where behaviors come from and how they are connected. You realize that the things you

138

don't like are connected to the things you do like. For example, America's ridiculous work ethics are connected to its relatively good organization and success, and Italy's work ethics are connected to its ability to appreciate people, food, and wine.

STAGE 4, ADAPTATION

You become familiar with the culture and how to get around. You learn to communicate better and relationships with your family improve. While you don't like the teaching style much, you've come to like your professors and have figured out how to get the information you need. You feel happier and more peaceful with your decision to study abroad. You're thankful for the opportunity.

STAGE 5, RECOVERY

You regain confidence and learn to appreciate the culture as a whole. You accept that which you cannot change, and find more good than evil. You may actually think the host culture is better than your own in many ways, and it may be hard to go home. You assimilate parts of the culture and feel renewed again.

MY STORY

When I first arrived in Cameroon, the Peace Corps staff picked us up from the airport and took us to a lovely little restaurant. It was the first time that I had ever tasted real mango juice. After lunch, they escorted us to the training camp, where a dance group welcomed us with drums and other traditional instruments. It felt good to be a part of the culture and experience so many changes all at once.

My host family was African-Muslim and Animist. They spoke both Fulfulde and French. Although I had taken two years of French in high school and college, I didn't speak well. Still I managed to communicate with my family and enjoy the new environment. It wasn't until a week or two later when I started getting distressed. I had fallen very sick and had to go outside to the latrine in the middle of the night.

On top of this, every time I turned on my flashlight to get up and go, there were two huge cockroaches crawling on the mosquito net above my head. There was also a very loud cricket somewhere in my bed that would suddenly start chirping every time I closed my eyes. I had to shake my sleeping bag to make it stop. Then fifteen minutes later, it would start again. It was exhausting and night after night, I just couldn't seem to get enough rest.

One night, I got up to go to the latrine and found a huge spider on my wall, probably about two inches wide and long. Not friendly with spiders, I threw my shoe from a distance, but it moved. I ended up piercing its big round sack belly, which I think was an egg, because out scurried hundreds of baby spiders. At that moment, I just covered my face and started sobbing. I felt like going home, but something inside convinced me to stay, and I did.

After this low point, I recovered from that terrible bout of diarrhea and learned how to manage the many bugs in my life. When I went to my site, I lived with strange flat spiders that suction-cupped the walls, mice that would raid my kitchen at night, tarantulas that partied under my bed, and a snake that took a liking to my oven. The cockroaches raided my latrine at night, and once, I even found a scorpion in my shoe.

HOW TO COPE

There are different ways of coping. While some ways are healthy and effective, others are unhealthy and ineffective. Avoiding the culture frequently and withdrawing on a consistent basis is ineffective. Coping is about finding balance and not allowing yourself to be distracted from what you came to accomplish. When our coping strategies cause us to lose track of personal and academic goals, they need to be re-evaluated.

Everyone has bad days, but what makes bad days worse is that you don't have your usual support systems. Nonetheless, there are a few things that you can do to help yourself get through. One of the best things is to get away by yourself for a while so that you can think clearly. Temporary occasional withdrawal is healthy and necessary to recharge your energy when you are culturally or linguistically challenged. Don't be too hard on yourself, and keep a healthy perspective.

After you've recharged, it's time to assert yourself and learn more about the culture. Join clubs and groups, put yourself in structured situations to get to know people, go out with your friends, spend time with your host family, and participate in extracurricular activities. Utilize resources through your study abroad program or institution to help you get started. Adaptability will help you have a successful experience abroad, and in many other turning points of your life.

Be an active learner, using knowledge to guide you through the experience. Dare your friends to venture outside of their worldviews and don't be afraid to do so yourself. Every culture has something valuable to offer. Strive to expand your identity, without losing or diluting your unique self. You don't have to become the culture; just allow the culture to make you a healthier and better person.

You can expect to miss some things from home, and this too is normal. It is hard to say what you'll miss the most; it really depends on your preferences. It may be McDonalds, it could be pizza, or it could be the mailbox. For me, it was carpet; I missed lying down on the floor. What you miss will depend on lots of things, namely the likeability and availability of certain things while you are abroad. In Cameroon, it was hard to find dairy products like ice cream and cheese. A few grocers carried it, but it was very expensive and didn't taste the same as it did back home.

Try to find something you like in the culture to counterbalance what you miss from home. In France, I had the most delicious crepes! Back in the United States, I was longing. It doesn't matter if you're here or there, you'll always miss something and you'll always be attached to what you have at the moment, whether you realize it or not. Generally, the more experiences you have in this life, the more you'll have to appreciate and subsequently crave when what you had before is long gone.

Many years ago, I received a post card advertisement from an Internet company called *Home Sick Snacks*. The advertisement read, "Your momma may be 5000 miles away, but homesicksnacks.com is just a click away." My colleagues and I got a kick out of that concept because we remembered those days of longing!

Write down what you miss in your journal. Someday you'll look back and appreciate how you've changed. It is good for the soul to yearn. It reminds us of our humanity and helps us put things in perspective.

68. Stereotypes and you

To travel is to discover that everyone is wrong about other countries. — Aldous Huxley

As with any large group of people, there are plenty of stereotypes about Americans: outgoing, loud, friendly, informal, egotistical, immature, hard-working, extravagant, wasteful, too confident, wealthy, disrespectful, preju-diced, ignorant of other countries, uninterested in foreign languages, gen-erous, always in a hurry, and oblivious of class or status. Many of these things are true, for certain populations and segments of the United States.

When I was living in Ecuador, my host family was lavishing me with im-ported canned foods from the United States. I didn't want to eat canned foods every day, so I asked them curiously why they weren't sharing their fresh green beans with me. As it turned out, my host mother was trying to make me happy. She thought that canned food would be easier on my stomach, since she presumed it was all that Americans are accustomed to eating. In those days, most foods imported from the United States came in cans.

So what is American culture and why don't we like to be stereotyped? Re-member, America was founded by individualists, the free thinkers and re-bels of the world! Remember also that not all America comes from an individualistic background; a good percentage of our people's ancestors were brought in against their will for the slave trade.

There are three Americas (North, Central, and South) with lots of countries throughout. Yet, when we say the word "American," what we really mean is someone from the United States. Other countries call themselves by their national title: *French* for France, *Spanish* for Spain, *Ecuadorian* for Ecuador, *Brazilian* for Brazil, *Mexican* for Mexico and *Canadian* for Canada, etc. United States is the only one that has an adjective for its people that does not stem from either the national language or the primary name of the country. This says something about our self-image. We are American, not United-*Statians*. America is the land of the free!

When we travel, others pigeonhole us by our race, gender, nationality, and religion. This is how they make sense of who we are in the context of their world. Race and gender is usually obvious, as we cannot hide physical characteristics. Nationality is somewhat of a guessing game, based on stereotypes—although I've noticed that one of the first questions people ask is where I'm from, even before they ask my name. Religion is sometimes visible and sometimes not, but people generally assume my religion once they know my nationality, race, etc. The dance continues as we try to step into each other's reality and mind.

Travel beckons our consciousness. The first travelers set out to discover new lands, but we set out to discover our real selves and each other. As an American woman, you may not see yourself as promiscuous, but that stereotype is pinned on your back, especially if you're young and pretty. Anyway, don't underestimate the power of your behavior to strengthen or weaken the stereotypes in the world. If enough people from a culture act differently, it will change the way the world sees them. Maybe someday men will say, "Those American women are really hard to get and smart, too!"

69. Anti-American sentiment

Be the change you want to see in the world. — Mahatma Gandhi

Anti-American sentiment is the feeling of opposition or unfriendliness toward the U.S. government, people, or culture. This usually comes from the perception that the United States is unilateral and responsive only to its own interests.

What is hard to get across is that Americans are not their government. Most Americans are just trying to make the best of life and want the best for their families and humankind. Many give to charity and provide time as well as money to those in need. Many like to travel and learn about other cultures and people.

Lots of Americans travel abroad without incident. Usually, civilized people do not like violence, and they don't like to hurt others, even when there is disagreement. Nonetheless, here are a few tips to help you guide your safety when it comes to anti-American sentiment:

Know what's going on around you at all times. Never drink more than you can stay alert.

Stay informed about U.S. foreign policy and how your host country has been affected by it.

Don't be defensive; listen to people and put things in perspective. Show them you understand.

Be open to other viewpoints to develop a more global perspective and understanding of worldviews.

Don't flaunt your Americanism in public. Keep a low profile when it comes to your nationality.

Avoid clothing and accessories that make you stand out as an American, since you never know who might be watching.

Avoid conversations about politics and religion in crowded public places where you can be overheard, and do not voice your opinions to the media.

Avoid demonstrations and other events where anti-American sentiments can be expressed and acknowledged.

Stay away from American hangouts and other establishments, as they are prime targets for terrorism and for identifying and trapping Americans.

If you sense anti-Americanism and someone asks you where you're from, you can always say that you're from Canada. Pick a city you're familiar with, like Toronto, or Quebec if you know some French.

Prejudice and discrimination is a widespread sickness that has infected every country in some way, shape, or form. This is because ignorance has great power in large groups. Even if you don't experience prejudice directly, you will experience it indirectly.

In many of the large, modern cities of Latin America, the *mestizos* (mixed Spanish-European) frown upon the *indigenous* (pure Indian). They are usually not cruel, in the sense that they spit on or attack others. Rather, they treat the indigenous people as uneducated, dishonest, and dirty, and they distance themselves physically and psychologically.

As a student, you have a unique opportunity to stand up to persecutors and stand up for the victims of discrimination. You can do this in small ways by befriending, respecting, honoring, and cherishing those who are persecuted, in plain view of those who do the persecuting.

70. Gender and experience

Sometimes I wonder if men and women really suit each other. Perhaps they should live next door and just visit now and then. — Katharine Hepburn

The rights, roles, and responsibilities of gender are unique in every country. When I was living and working in Cameroon, the character and strength of the everyday African woman was amazing. She farmed under the hot sun, cooked, cleaned, and cared for many children. Her arms and legs were strong, and bigger than those of her husband. She was generous, friendly, capable, and joyous. Her attitudes and behaviors commanded nothing but my utmost respect. Sadly, she had to deal with many abuses, such as husbands drinking in bars and cheating on their wives openly with prostitutes, and the spread of HIV.

It was truly heartbreaking to see women degraded by abuse imposed on their gender. In one case, my friend's husband passed away, and she was forced by tradition to sleep with her dead husband's body for seven days. She wasn't allowed to bathe, wash, or even change her bloody menstrual cloth during that period. In other African tribes and the Middle East, an estimated 125 million women have had clitoridectomies in 29 countries, in the name of religion and culture.[10] The Chinese practiced foot binding (also known as "Lotus feet"), a painful process to stop the feet of young girls from growing, crippling them for life.

Although more countries have permitted women to rise into positions of power, the masses haven't changed their attitudes and behaviors toward women. Chile, Bolivia, Argentina, Liberia, the Philippines, Panama, Ireland, Iceland, and more have all seen women presidents, but they are not egalitarian or even close to it. Women are still produced, packaged, and played all over the world. This is man trying to tame women like they do animals, for their own pleasures and purposes.

How your gender factors into your experience will depend on many circumstances. If you are a woman, you may be expected to follow the same rules, but you may also have a free pass because you are not a part of the

---

[10] Female Genital Mutilation/Cutting: A Global Concern. UNICEF, New York, 2016.

culture. I was not treated as African women were treated; I was treated differently and in social contexts with much more respect because of where I came from and the color of my skin.

While the African men seemed to grant me more freedom and respect in social contexts, they were always trying to wiggle their way into more. This is because American women have a reputation of being easy. If you are a woman traveler, you must have simple but firm boundaries and you must know how to say no. If you are a person who doesn't like to say no, then it may be uncomfortable for you in the beginning. However, the more you practice taking care of yourself, the easier it becomes.

71. Avoiding unwanted attention

The road to truth is long, and lined the entire way with annoying bastards. — Alexander Jablokov

In certain areas of the world, behaviors associated with gender equality may be interpreted as promiscuous by the local men. Things like making eye contact, and smiling in a way that you consider friendly or polite, can mean "Come on, Baby," to a local man who is not accustomed to communicating with American women. Just wearing shorts in some areas of the world can label you as a prostitute. Check out journeywoman.com, just for women.

As for unwanted attention, the best thing you can do is ignore it. If someone grabs you, pull away and project an attitude of confidence and authority. When I worked for the Peace Corps, I was harassed daily. If I responded, they'd harass me more. If I ignored it, they'd either leave me alone, or on rare occasions grab me. In this case, I'd pull away, squint my eyes, straighten my back, tighten up my shoulders, curl my hands into fists, and reveal my teeth with a snarl. It worked beautifully.

In addition to being a study abroad professional, I was also a self-defense instructor. So if anyone ever attacks you, I can safely say that the first thing you should do is scream. Pulling back fingers, poking eyes, kicking a shin, grabbing some hair, scratching a face, and twisting ears all cause an attacker to feel pain. In pain, he is more likely to let go of you. At that point, run for help. Never go to a secondary location with an attacker. Most likely, the attacker has a sick, perverted, or angry intention to rape or kill you; otherwise, he wouldn't be trying to take you somewhere else.

72. Friendship, dating, and marriage

Friendship is born at that moment when one person says to another: "What! You, too? Thought I was the only one." — C.S. Lewis

In many parts of the world, the friendship and dating scene is similar to that of your home country. However, expectations and expressions may be different. You may be expected to behave and not behave in certain ways towards good friends and dates. For example, in parts of Africa, same-sex friends hold hands in public, as a symbol of their friendship. It's not uncommon to see two male friends, or two female friends, walking hand-in-hand and being touchy-feely with each other.

Before you grab your friend's hand though, you had better know the customs. Another thing to be careful about is showing affection in public with the opposite sex. In several parts of the world, namely Japan and Cameroon, expressing any kind of public affection between the sexes is forbidden. However, in other parts of the world, you'll see quite the opposite. In Latin America, for example, certain parks are full of couples making out and sometimes doing a lot more. You get used to seeing it after a while and just turn the other way.

You should also know about flirting in your host culture. Eye contact can be a sign of interest. If you're a woman and a man is buying you drinks at a bar, the expectation could be that you agree to sleep with him later in the night. If you're a man and you're visiting a local woman's home after dark, it may mean that you want to get sexual. A man once shook my hand, and wiggled his finger inside, like he was tickling my palm. I thought it was strange and later learned that he was asking me to sleep with him. If I had wiggled my finger back, then I would have agreed.

If you are interested in pursuing a romantic relationship with a local, then you should know how to do it right. If you're a man, is it customary to walk your date to the door and give her a kiss goodnight? In many parts of the world, such an act could be pushy and overbearing, wanting sex en lieu of love. You may be surprised to know that in some countries, like Australia and New Zealand, women often pick up the tab. In Arab countries, there isn't much dating, and a marriage proposal requires a very large down payment to the family of the bride.

In some cultures, dating is a family affair; the two families take time to befriend and approve of each other way before a marriage takes place. India has a long tradition of arranged marriages; perhaps this is why it has the lowest divorce rate in the world. The United States tends to see marriage as a closed system, between two people. This is interesting, since we have one of the highest divorce rates.

While hard to believe, there was no such thing as dating in the early ages. Men would raid villages and capture women they wanted for wives. Dating was born from the concept of chivalry in medieval times. Still, it wasn't about romance, it was about finding women who could have children and help with the workload. This is why it was traditional for the male counterparts to pay on a date. It wasn't until later that dating grew into something romantic. Actually, before 1228 it was against the law for women to propose marriage.

QUICK FACTS ON DATING AND FRIENDSHIP CUSTOMS

In Iran, it's illegal to date.

In Afghanistan, dating is rare because parents arrange most marriages.

In Russia, it is customary to ask the parents for a woman's hand.

In Australia, women often ask out men and pay for the date.

In the Philippines, when a man decides to wed a woman, his parents usually visit her house and present an extravagant gift first.

In some parts of Europe, dating is usually a group event (i.e. Finland).

In parts of Europe, Greenland, Asia, the Middle East, and Africa, same-sex affection is presumed to be friendship, not homosexuality.

In Northern Africa and the Middle East, opposite-sex friendships and homosexuality are shunned.

In Spain, dating is a one-on-one event and both parties ask each other out and share costs.

In parts of East Asia, only men ask and pay.

In Native American cultures, blood-brotherhood rituals are common.

In East Asia, young people don't date until they go to college, or are in their mid-20s.

In India, dating is serious business for permanent relationships, not just for fun.

In France, it is common for women to share the tab with their date.

In Ukraine, men offer women their arms, not their hands. Men and women in general do not hold hands.

In most of the world, friendship is a serious commitment. There are formal friendship rituals in many African cultures.

Getting married overseas is romantic and exciting, but not without head-aches. You and your fiancé will need to present specific documentation, and then after you marry, you'll have to figure out how to get residency. If your spouse is returning to the United States, apply for permanent residency. Information is available from the Bureau of Citizenship and Immigration Services in the Department of Homeland Security. If you are planning to stay in the host country, you will need to get a residency card from the ap-propriate government office.

According to Title 22, Code of Federal Regulations 52.1, American diplo-matic and consular officers are not permitted to perform marriages abroad. This regulation exists primarily because the laws of a country govern the legal agreement of marriage. Hence, it makes sense that Argentina's civil and religious officials perform a marriage ceremony that takes place in Ar-gentina, between an Argentinean and an American citizen. As for docu-mentation, you will typically need to present an affidavit from the U.S. em-bassy stating that you are not presently married in your country, and you are legally capable of entering into a marriage contract.

Marriages of U.S. citizen(s) abroad are always registered in the country where they occur. The U.S. government doesn't play part in the registration of marriages overseas. Be sure to bring a few copies of your certificate home with you if returning to the United States permanently. It will usually be accepted as official evidence. If it is written in a foreign language, the re-quester of evidence may require an official translation. The U.S. govern-ment can authenticate your foreign marriage documents for a fee, but it's not required.

The best source of information about marriage in a particular country is the tourist information bureau of that country and the American embassy or consulate. In some countries, there are two separate ceremonies. I was mar-ried in Ecuador where a legal ceremony is viewed as a semi-commitment, and a religious ceremony is a serious, lifelong endeavor. Many people will marry in the law to see how things go for a few years before having a reli-gious ceremony.

Name-change customs are also very interesting. In many Latin American countries, for example, women keep their maiden name and add on their husband's name. Both husband and wife have their spouse's name written on the back of their government identification card. Also, children take the last names of both their mother and father.

73. Alcohol and drugs

Alcohol removes inhibitions – like that scared little mouse who got drunk and shook his whiskers and shouted: "Now bring on that damn cat!" — Eleanor Early

Never, ever use illegal drugs in a foreign country. If you choose to consume alcoholic beverages, always do so legally and appropriately. Also, know that you don't have to drink alcohol in order to be culturally appropriate. If you don't drink for whatever reason (religion, addiction, nutrition, medication), it's okay. Many people don't drink alcohol or beverages with caffeine because they are taking anti-depressants or other medications. You don't have to specify why you choose not to drink, just say it's for personal reasons.

If you choose to drink alcohol legally, in accordance with the laws of the host country, there are some social and cultural implications to consider. In many areas of the world, alcoholic beverages are a part of everyday life. In West Africa, it's palm wine or corn beer; in Europe, it's grape wine; and in Latin America, it's sangria, made from a variety of fruit. Especially in Europe, fine wine is viewed as sacred, and will likely accompany meals, social gatherings, and other celebrations; drunkenness is not tolerated, and people don't have the desire or need to drink excessively.

When consuming alcohol, drink slowly and drink with food. One drink per hour, with food, is a good formula. Never drink more than four glasses per hour. Also, know the potency (proof) of whatever you drink. Obviously, a glass of tequila will go farther than a glass of wine. Beer in other countries may be a lot stronger than it is at home, not to mention the big bottles.

Don't drink alone. If you or someone else is drinking alone, it may be a sign of depression, an emotional problem, or an addiction. If you think you have a problem with alcohol, get help. Warning: Alcohol is one of the most widely used social drugs in the world and affects the mind and body. In short, it raises blood pressure and triglycerides; impairs judgment, reflexes, and coordination; and displaces nutrients from the body after consumption. Research also links alcohol use to brain damage, heart damage, nerve damage, stomach inflammation and bleeding, tremors, dementia, stroke, cancer, malnutrition, hepatitis, liver disease, cirrhosis, obesity, and more. Do not use alcohol during pregnancy and in case of other medical conditions, as recommended by your Doctor.

Age Limit	Countries
No age limit	China, Poland, Thailand, Vietnam
21	United States
20	Japan, Iceland
19	South Korea

18	Argentina, Australia, Barbados, Brazil, Chile, Canada (age 19 in some provinces), Czech Republic, Ecuador, Hong Kong, Israel, Malaysia, Mexico, New Zealand, Peru, Philippines, Puerto Rico, Ukraine, U.K. (16 in restaurants), Russia, South Africa, Venezuela
16	Austria, Belgium, Italy, France, Germany, Greece, Netherlands, Norway, Poland, Spain, Switzerland, Turkey

MAXIMIZE YOUR STAY

74. Get informed

All things are ready, if our mind be so. — William Shakespeare

Indeed, one of the best ways to maximize your stay is to learn as much as you can about where you are, while you're there.

People from other countries tend to follow world events more closely than people from the United States. If you don't know what's going on in the world, then you won't have much to contribute to conversations with people who do. Don't foster the stereotype of the uninformed American; follow international news online through world-newspapers.com.

It's also important that you follow local news. Buy the newspaper and watch the local television stations. Become an informed member of your community and get passionate about things that are going on. I participated in a few community meetings back when Matteo Renzi was the mayor of Florence. I met him personally and watched the community try to resolve several problems with him. It was exciting to see him in action early in his career and later as he went on to become Prime Minister of Italy.

75. Immerse yourself

Nothing in life is to be feared. It is only to be understood. — Marie Curie

By discovering a new culture, you can become more enlightened, but the only way to do it right is to jump in and immerse yourself. Some aspects of this process will be liberating and others will be frustrating, particularly inefficiencies and antiquated practices. Eventually, you will find a balance that works for you, and it will help you grow into a better, more open-minded human being.

I joined the Peace Corps because I wanted to make a difference in people's lives while simultaneously learning from them. I don't remember if I was trying to be cynical or if I sincerely wanted to know, but I asked my host mother how to take a bath in a bucket, since that's the way they bathed with no running water. To my surprise, she striped me naked and washed me. This was one of the most embarrassing moments of my adult life.

As the days passed, my host family taught me how to wash my clothes, iron, cook, fetch water from the well, collect rainwater in a big barrel to avoid trips to the well, and a whole horde of other skills. I didn't know how to do anything without the luxuries of modern-day technology, which made me feel vulnerable. My African host family and all of my African friends taught me more about life than I could have ever taught them, unless baking banana bread and chocolate-chip cookies counts for something.

I've alluded to this before, but before I became a Peace Corps Volunteer, I thought that the United States was superior to the rest of the world. Lesson learned: there isn't *better* when it comes to culture, there is just *different*. The only "better" is learning to adapt to the differences in a positive and successful way.

76. Be patient with yourself

Patience is bitter, but its fruit is sweet. — Aristotle

Be patient with yourself. Don't expect to understand everything all at once. Learning language and culture take time.

I didn't know how to speak French or Spanish before going to the Peace Corps, but after about a year in each country, I was able to hold a conversation and get around without any problem. Now, after having lived in Italy for two years, I speak Italian. Currently, I'm working with some Italian authors to translate and publish their work in English.

A semester or year may seem like a long time, but one thing that students always tell me is that their experiences weren't long enough. In the end, they wish they'd had more time. Logistically, planning for a year and deciding to come back early is much easier than planning for a semester and later deciding to stay for a year.

77. Be vulnerable

Because he could not afford to fail, he could not afford to trust.
— Joseph J. Ellis, His Excellency: George Washington

Being vulnerable means not being afraid to try new things and make mistakes. Have a sense of humor about yourself and laugh! When I was in Ecuador, my former mother-in-law asked me if I liked *jugo de carne*, which literally means *meat juice*. Having no clue what I was about to receive (at worse, a glass of blood with my rice and beans); I received a plate of delicious beef stew with homegrown tomatoes.

Don't be afraid to ask when you don't understand something. For most people, helping others makes them feel wanted and needed, and gives them purpose in life. As a foreigner, you're at an advantage because people don't expect you to know everything. When you ask a question, you open opportunities for connection and conversation. Others jump in and your question suddenly turns into a thought-provoking group discussion.

Too many people are afraid to fail. They don't want to lose, so they don't play the game, but who doesn't play sports because they're afraid of losing? It's true, when you're vulnerable, you can be misunderstood, falsely labeled, criticized, attacked, and worst of all, rejected. So many times I have looked stupid, incompetent, and downright crazy. Quitting my job and moving my whole family to Italy took the cake, and believe me, I had to face a lot of challenges and issues in that decision. Still though, I do not regret it. I feel thankful and blessed to have had the experience.

Being vulnerable expands your world; it gives you life and freedom like you can never imagine. In a way, it's the beginning of a brave new you, a decision to be who you are, allowing other people see who you are, no matter the cost. It takes courage and it's hard, but there's big benefits in stepping out of your comfort zone. So many people live in caves, never seeing the light outside, never knowing who they are, and what they really want out of life. Let yourself go.

78. Learn the art of language

Language is the dress of thought. — Samuel Johnson

Imagine sitting in a coffee shop, in Chicago, when someone approaches and asks you a question in Chinese. You don't speak Chinese, and a variety of thoughts race through your mind. *He must not speak any English at all. How can that be since he's obviously in the USA for one reason or another? What in the world is he trying to say to me?* You may want to help him, or you may tell him, "No Chinese" and send him away. Either way, you probably think he should at least know a few words and phrases in English since he's in your country. He didn't even try to speak it.

Don't make a bad first impression of yourself or your country by not speaking enough of the host language to get around the city that you're visiting. People are willing to help, especially when you can show some appreciation of their language and culture. Even if the language is not widely spoken, and even if everyone speaks English, you should still learn some phrases. You may notice that the locals speak their own language with each other and insiders, and English to outsiders. Learning the language will improve your relationships and experience. It will get you on the inside of the fence, where you can really grow.

I hope that you have a small dictionary with vital words and phrases. Put sticky notes on everything in your home, with the written word in the host language, and carry around flashcards. Take advantage of language classes and any tutoring offered by your school. Listen to the radio, watch television shows with subtitles, and read local newspapers. Write down the lyrics of popular songs and read children's stories in the host language. Practice speaking aloud, even when you study by yourself, and don't be afraid to make mistakes. Form sentences with different verb tenses.

Sure, you'll mess up, but it's okay; that's why humans were created with a sense of humor. When I was learning Spanish, I told my host family that I was *pregnant*, rather than *embarrassed*; "Estoy embarazada" means "I'm pregnant" in Spanish. I was dating their son, so we had a good laugh about it. Lighten up; have a sense of humor about yourself and you'll feel better. Knowing another language not only improves your overall communication, but it can enhance cognitive ability not related to language and prevent dementia in old age.[11]

While we like to think of language as being written and spoken words, we need to consider other aspects of language as well. These are non-verbal and include greetings, gestures, eye contact, personal space, facial expressions, posture, touching, and behaviors, which take on different meanings across cultures. You should know the major differences to avoid embarrassing and offensive mistakes. For example, a thumbs-up gesture in the Middle East is very vulgar and offensive. Thus, you would not want to inadvertently give any Middle Easterner a thumbs-up in any country.

We cannot discuss language without also mentioning the fact that in most Western cultures, speaking is more important than listening. In fact, it's a skill. Success and leadership in Western culture is directly linked to the ability to speak well. This makes most Westerners passive listeners, since the speaker motivates the process. In many non-Western cultures, however, listening is an active form of the communication process. Active listeners are internally motivated; they do not need speakers to help them listen. Listening is the skill; not speaking.

There are subtle nuances in language, communication, and culture. If you take the time to study them, observe, listen, and understand, you can become an excellent cross-cultural communicator.

---

[11] Yudhijit Bhattacharjee, "Why Bilinguals are Smarter," New York Times, March 17, 2010.

Translation Bloopers (for fun)

The Dairy Association's success with the *Got Milk?* campaign ended up in Mexico, but it didn't do so well because in Spanish it read "Are You Lactating?"

A sign in an Italian Laundromat translated as "Ladies, leave your clothes here and have a good time."

In China, Pepsi's slogan *Come Alive* translated into "Pepsi Brings Your Ancestors Back from the Grave."

The Dairy Association's success with the *Got Milk?* campaign ended up in Mexico, but it didn't do so well because in Spanish it read "Are You Lactating?"

A sign in an Italian Laundromat translated as "Ladies, leave your clothes here and have a good time."

In China, Pepsi's slogan *Come Alive* translated into "Pepsi Brings Your Ancestors Back from the Grave."

A detour sign in Japan reads "Stop: Drive Sideways."

Gerber baby food wasn't doing well in Africa, with a smiling baby on the label. Later the company learned that in Africa, pictures on the label often indicate what's inside, since many people can't read.

An advertisement for donkey rides in Thailand reads, "Would you like to ride on your own ass?"

79. Don't be afraid of obstacles

The traveler sees what he sees. The tourist sees what he has come to see. — G.K. Chesterton

You will no doubt face obstacles in your journey abroad. Obstacles are the things that make you grow; you cannot change without them. The best way to get through hard times is to open your mind and allow yourself to see the good in all people and things. Find in other cultures what suits you better than your own and integrate it into your life.

Seek the journey, not the destination. You certainly want to see all you can, but not at the sacrifice of experience. If you hop on a tourist bus that stops at twenty different sites in only a few hours, then you miss the authentic and real experience of walking the streets, browsing shops, watching people socialize in crowded squares, and dining in local cafés. Conquering destinations is just a form of showing off.

One of the things I admire about some countries and their people is that they know how to live. The systems may not be as smooth and efficient, but the quality of life is higher, and relationships mean more. People make time to stroll, smell the roses, visit with loved ones, and experience the nuances of life like food, arts, etc. I like to take at least one day per week to meander with a map and some money. With no plans, I let destiny carry me that day, within reason. I try to live in the moment and enjoy.

Happy people, no matter what the circumstances, find joy within themselves. It was joyfulness that drove you to study abroad, and it's perseverance that will get you through the difficult times. Keep your head high and your feet on the path, never really arriving to your destination. In this way, your life will stay interesting and you'll get through the hard times with more grace. You won't be afraid of obstacles because you'll realize that obstacles are really blessings that help you see and grow.

80. Live like a local

The traveler was active; he went strenuously in search of people, of adventure, of experience. The tourist is passive; he expects interesting things to happen to him. He goes "sight-seeing."
— Daniel J. Boorstin

When I was abroad, I met many missionaries from America and Europe that lived way above the standard of the locals, with modern homes, SUVs, etc. In particular, I remember a European couple who built and ran a new health center in my small African village. When I asked a local friend why people weren't going to the center, she replied, "Come on, Wendy! Their dogs (the pets of the doctor and his wife) eat better than our children." This spoke to me, loud and clear; we have to be willing to get into other people's shoes if we want to walk with them. If you can't live at least somewhat like the locals, you'll have a tough time relating with them and will miss much of their culture.

81. Take healthy risks

When we allow ourselves to become vulnerable, to take chances, and to risk our pride, that is when we find our own glory. — Richard Corman

Think about a risk you took in your life and what it did for you. Even if it didn't have the outcome you were expecting, it probably taught you some valuable lesson. In fact, small, healthy risks improve the quality of your life when they don't result in misfortune that can happen anywhere. Not long ago, a woman who had traveled around the world was in a grocery store in a small city in Indiana. A man went into the store with a gun, to threaten his girlfriend who worked there. There was a fight and the innocent woman was shot and killed. Who would have thought that traveling around the world would be safe for her, and going to the grocery store at home would have ended her life?

A risk for one person is not the same for another. Your risk may be simply saying "Hello" to someone or going to the market by yourself. It may be deciding to study abroad or it may be deciding to go to college abroad. We take risks every single day. The woman who was shot in the grocery store took a risk when she left her house to buy some food. But she would have taken a different risk to stay home. Strangely, in the same week, another man who was running from the police, found himself in a neighborhood, trying to get into someone's house.

You'll know when a risk is worth taking because you will feel incredibly sorry and guilty if you decide not to take it. You will feel like you are stopping your whole life for a delusion of comfort and security. A risk is nothing more than giving up one form of comfort and security for something else that is unsure. What is life if we don't take chances? If we are not willing to budge from our comfort zones, we lose the opportunity for a richer and fuller existence.

82. Read and write

Journal writing is a voyage to the interior. — Christina Baldwin

Read historic or contemporary novels, identify great figures that traveled the same road, choose a new-founded hero, and follow this hero on a journey of discovery. If you're in Paris, read *Hemingway: The Paris Years* by Michael S. Reynolds, and experience what it's like to live in Hemingway's Paris. Read works by Elizabeth Hamilton or Jane Porter in Great Britain. Going to South Africa? Read *Cry, the Beloved Country* by Alan Paton. If Cameroon, Ecuador, or France are on your bucket list, or you're contemplating the Peace Corps, read my fiction debut: *Love Evil: An extraordinary journey of the heart.*

Keep a journal and blog if you are able. Blogging is harder to preserve for keepsake and you can't get too personal. You may also not be able to access the Internet to blog as frequently as you can jot things down in a journal. I have lots of pictures, personal letters, and journals from my Peace Corps days, but since the email revolution, I can't get organized enough to save my e-thoughts and e-ideas for memories anymore. I can't even get organized enough to print digital photographs on a regular basis. There is just too much information to manage now.

Journaling is not a time-consuming process of summarizing your experiences day after day; I'm talking about recording memories in a systematic way that enables you to find information ten years later. Instead of writing from front to back, divide your journal into four sections to safeguard your memories. Consider a binder-style notebook with dividers where you can add pages.

THE FOUR SECTIONS
People – Use this section to record information about friends, professors, host family, significant others, strangers, people you are keeping in contact with back home, etc. Leave the first page blank for a table of contents and fill the rest of the pages with personal information like full name, how you met each other, birthday, address, phone, and your relationship. Paste in photos, email messages, etc.

Facts – This section is reserved for facts you want to recall in the future like recipes, foods you liked, places you visited, where you attended school, your address and phone in the host country, bizarre foods, stores you want to remember, restaurants you enjoy, trains, hostels, airlines, holidays, routes, unique words you learn, museums, historic sites and their significance, etc. You can draw pictures and maps, too, or paste them in.

Ahha's – Questions, thoughts, feelings, discoveries, ideas, and cultural differences, which come to you as a result of your study abroad experience. It's how you change mentally, emotionally, intellectually, spiritually, and physically. It's your record of transformation. Use it for joyfulness, frustration, humility, pride, anger, etc. Whenever your writing is motivated by deep thoughts and feelings, it should go here.

Activity – Reserve this section for activities and stories. Do you want to remember a day in the life? Or, did something exciting, hilarious, or bizarre happen to you? An activity may be your everyday walk to school. A story could be an annual festival, a trip to Auschwitz, a child you befriended, a good time with friends, an embarrassing moment, your personal experience with a historical event, or a journey to the rain forest. Stories are what make our experiences come alive to other people.

Consider bringing a few glue sticks to paste memoirs into your journal like photographs, tickets, etc. Don't throw away your maps; mark where you live, the paths you walk, where you go to school, the places you visited in other cities, the routes you followed, etc. You can use a color-code system to distinguish routes and locations. Over time, you may forget this information and be thankful you have a record. If you don't have a city map, then draw one with a pen. In addition to your journal, get a small binder to keep your maps and categorize them.

83. Value people

...there is nothing in the world as interesting as people, and one can never study them enough.
— Vincent Van Gogh

The real beauty of international travel is not the places we see, but the people we meet. It's through our relationships that we give and take, and subsequently change, which can be for better or worse. Consequently, it's important to connect with the right people who can help you grow and change in a positive direction.

Look for similarities. Friends have characteristics that pull them together like values, hobbies, work, and goals. Try to find at least three or four things that you have in common. This will keep the relationship alive, while all the differences allow you both to grow in new directions. Similarities and differences are the beauty of relationships. Some combinations work really well together, and some don't.

Be transparent and real with people. Don't put on a façade and pretend you're someone that you are not, otherwise you'll end up with a bunch of incompatible, fake friends. There is nothing worse than being stuck in fake-mode during such an important time in your life. Get over yourself as an object of other people's approval. Appreciate and love who you are.

Share yourself with others. People are usually as interested in you and your culture as you are in theirs. When I was living with my African family, my host mother often saw me doing push-ups, as I was a workout fanatic. One thing led to another and before I knew it, I was teaching my African mama martial arts. She did a few moves and we all laughed. I wrote about this in my book *Love Evil*, where I highlight many of my real-life experiences.

Since listening in a foreign language means you're constantly translating in your mind, it's easy to get tired and start daydreaming. Try to avoid this by letting your host family and friends know when you are mentally worn out and just need a break. Always give 100% of your attention; don't be afraid to seek clarification when you don't understand, and never pretend to understand what you don't or it may come back to haunt you.

Expect and accept differences. Everyone is both different and similar to you in some way. It's okay. Agree to disagree and focus on the things you have in common and the things that excite you about the other person. Most married couples are opposite in many ways; one is always hot while the other is cold, or one is outgoing while the other is a homebody. If the relationship works, then they must think the benefits outweigh the detriments or they wouldn't stay together. It's important to realize that differences are compulsory for personal growth.

Finally, step into other people's shoes. When you step out of your own experience, and into another, you learn and grow, but you also nourish that relationship. You can learn a lot about others by doing things their way. Show interest in just getting to know people and what makes them tick. Visit their homes, eat what they like to eat, etc. There's nothing more honorable than when people show interest and curiosity in who you are.

84. Engage globally

There's enough on this planet for everyone's needs but not for everyone's greed.
— Mahatma Gandhi

One of the greatest transformations that this world has seen can be summed up with one word: *globalization*. Globalization is the wide-reaching integration of economic, cultural, and political systems. For the first time in history, a ripple in one major economy can shake the entire world. Read *The World is Flat* by Thomas Friedman, for a big-picture perspective.

Since the world is evolving into one system, it is important that we learn how to manage it for the good of people and the planet. Although we are globally dependent, we don't have enough awareness, knowledge, and skill to effectively manage our future. It's our mismanagement of everything that has created an array of global issues. If we don't deal with and effectively resolve these issues, then we will eventually see our demise.

Given the vast number of global issues, and how they're all interconnected, nations must work together on resolutions. Take some time during your study abroad experience to learn about some of these issues and get involved with solutions. Problem solving experience and the actual skills are very good for your resume and life. Here are five broad areas to consider:

CONFLICT AND ABUSE
This includes violence, terrorism, guerrilla activities, war, arms trafficking, weapons of mass destruction (biological, chemical, nuclear), ethnic cleans-

ing, and genocide both within nations and between nations of the world, gender power, abuse of women and children, sex trafficking, prostitution, ethnic-racial-political-religious abuse, and government corruption.

Ideologies, philosophies, and religions are deeply embedded in culture and politics. To understand more about conflict and abuse, and to influence change, study major world religions, political philosophies, and cultural ideologies. A good understanding of human diversity will help you to develop strategies for reducing stereotypes, prejudice, and discrimination, as well as solve problems that stem from ethnic and racial tensions.

ECONOMY AND PLANET

This includes trade politics, currency exchange rates, foreign assistance barriers, national and foreign debt, the failing of the global financial system, exportation of jobs, rising economic disparity (between rich and poor), environmental pollution, natural resource depletion, ozone depletion, toxic and nuclear waste, deforestation, acid rain, global warming, environmental disasters, climate change, drought, and species eradication.

Learn about alternative energy sources and conservation. Familiarize yourself with the UN, NATO, SEATO, OAS, and OAU. Study alliances, such as NAFTA, treaties, and negotiations, devolution of the nations, political disintegration, secessionism, separatism, irredentism, and the opposing trends of regional integration and increased democratization. Solutions lie in redistributing wealth, bringing back the gold standard for currencies, promoting fair trade, and guarding biodiversity and natural resources.

LIFE AND QUALITY OF LIFE

This includes lack of health care, food shortages, nutrition deficits, massive famines, infectious diseases, inadequate sanitation, drug use and abuse (trade, prevention, prosecution), inadequate shelter and housing, illiteracy, shrinking economic resources, lack of social safety nets, illegal aliens, high populations in the cities, political asylum, dependency ratios (percentage of population under 15 or over 65 years old), mounting numbers of refugees worldwide, growing crime, and identity theft.

Research and gather data on growth, patterns, movements, and trends in populations around the world. Examine the role of science and technology in the lives of all human beings. Discover the causes of poverty to find solutions. Practice sustainable development.

A hot topic in study abroad is sustainable travel. If you want to learn more about how you can leave the world a better place, then look into Sustainable Travel International, a 501(c)(3) non-profit organization whose mission is to promote sustainable development and responsible international travel: sustainabletravel.org.

INTERNATIONAL DEVELOPMENT

This includes increasing foreign debt as well as economic imperialism, explosive urban growth in the cities (megacities) which overpower countries, cartels among developing nations that possess raw materials needed by industrialized nations, international security, and immigration.

Look into why such problems are happening and how they interconnect with other global issues. Research how solving one global issue (like the redistribution of wealth) could impact international developments and relationships.

MULTINATIONAL ORGANIZATIONS

United Nations (UN) – This international organization strives to solve problems that challenge humanity. It was founded in 1945 to stop wars between nations and to provide a platform for dialogue.

UN Education, Scientific, and Cultural Organization (UNESCO) – A specialized UN agency that promotes international cooperation among its Member States and Associate Members in the fields of education, science, culture and communication: unesco.org.

The World Bank Group – The World Bank is a vital source of financial and technical assistance to developing countries around the world. Its primary focus is to help the poorest of the poor. It is one of the largest sources of funding for the developing world: worldbank.org.

World Health Organization (WHO): who.int

World Trade Organization (WTO): wto.org

85. Make a difference

Too often travel, instead of broadening the mind, merely lengthens the conversation.
— Elizabeth Drew

When you decided to take a leap of faith and study abroad, you were probably focused on what it could do for you, and rightfully so. It is my sincere hope that you have a wonderful, life-changing experience, but this experience affects more than just you. Nobody knows yet how your presence will change the lives of other people in your network. You can only hope and try to be a positive influence.

One of the things we like to talk about in higher education is global citizenship. It's our hope that international education will cultivate this attitude-behavior in participants. A global citizen has a sense of responsibility. The person cares for human beings and the world, supports the well-being of others, works to alleviate global inequality, and avoids actions that harm people and the planet.

Global citizens feel a sense of belonging to a world community. They see beyond national borders to bigger problems. Globalcitizen.org is an online community of people who want to learn about and take action on the world's biggest challenges.

STUDY ABROAD MAP

GOING HOME

86. Saying proper goodbyes

Don't cry because it's over. Smile because it happened. — Dr. Seuss

When I left Cameroon, I didn't know that I wasn't returning. I was medically evacuated to the Peace Corps headquarters in Washington DC, and while away, the Peace Corps decided to close my post for safety reasons. Later, they offered me a new assignment in Ecuador, and I never had the opportunity to say goodbye to friends.

I wrote letters to some of my Cameroonian and Peace Corps friends, but it wasn't the same, and I never experienced closure in that part of my life. Had I known that I would not be returning, I would have said my goodbyes, acquired permanent contact information to keep in touch, taken more photos, organized my personal possessions, and given away many gifts.

I always thought that one day I would return to Cameroon, but it hasn't happened yet, and I don't know if it ever will. The lesson I took from this experience is that things can change quickly. Life has a way of taking turns, and with all good intentions, you may not have the opportunity to go back, at least not for a long time.

It's important to bring a certain closure to your relationships, even if you will be in touch via email, and do so in a culturally appropriate manner. It may be expected that you give gifts, or that you have a goodbye party. Your goodbyes are final impressions in people's hearts and minds. Be sure to say goodbye to everyone, even to the store clerks and the bus drivers.

87. Returning with gifts

Every gift from a friend is a wish for your happiness. — Richard Bach

Good international gifts capture the essence of the location. If the country or city is known to have beautiful wall art, then a small painting might be nice. If you're in southern France, get *Herb de Provence* or *Savon de Marseille*. It also depends on how many family members and friends you're shopping for, how much space you have in your luggage, and how careful you can be with fragile items. Packing Tip: If transporting fragile items, wrap them up in clothing and put them in the middle of your bag.

Think about the size and weight of your gifts; you can't bring everything with you. If you're not running an import-export business, you probably have $800 of duty-free personal exemption, depending on the country. You can bring more; you just have to pay duty on it. Make certain you know before you go, so that you aren't stuck with a large bill.

Keep in mind that several items are prohibited or restricted. Alcohol is restricted to only a certain number of bottles. Fruit and meat are prohibited. The U.S. Customs and Border Protection department publishes a *Know*

Before You Go brochure and details everything on their website. Be sure to have a look.

88. Immigration and customs

A simple way to take measure of a country is to look at how many want in, and how many want out. — Tony Blair

You will either fill out a *declaration form* on the airplane or electronically once you arrive. You have to declare everything you are taking home that you didn't take with you before you went. Whether you bought the items or they were given to you as gifts, the same rules apply. Keep receipts and sales slips. State what you paid for each item, including tax. If you received a gift, then you need to estimate the fair market value. Be sure to pack declared items in a way that you can easily access them if necessary.

At your first port of entry in the USA, you will go through two processes before you either walk out of the airport or catch your next flight. The first is immigration. They will check to make sure that you, as a person, are okay to enter the country. You will then have to go to the baggage claim, grab a cart, pick up your checked luggage on a conveyer belt, and carry it through U.S. Customs.

It is the U.S. Customs who make sure that you're not bringing anything illegal into the country and that you pay duty that may be owed. Customs officials have the right to search you and your luggage. Even if they don't check your bags, they often have dogs that sniff for drugs. Penalties for lying to government officials are stiff, so be truthful.

Do customs officials know if you bought something outside of the United States? Well, they don't know for sure but they have the right to presume. The burden of proof is on you. For example, if you bought a camera in the

United States that was made in Japan, then you may have to pay duty on it unless you can prove you owned it before you went on your journey. Legitimate proof would be an official document such as a receipt, insurance policy, appraisal, etc. Once you get past Customs, you'll drop off your luggage again and proceed.

89. Reverse culture shock

The whole object of travel is not to set foot on foreign land; it is at last to set foot on one's own country as a foreign land. — G.K. Chesterton

After you return from your amazing journey, and go back to your everyday routine at home, you may experience *reverse culture shock*. You'll know if you feel frustrated, alienated, and misunderstood.

Maybe nobody mentioned it, but international education has a way of uprooting you permanently from home. Home is lost, and you're not likely to find it again in the way it existed before. This is because home is not where you come from; it's where you feel comfortable, more comfortable than anywhere else.

You will go through different stages of adjustment when returning home, just as you went through abroad. At first, it will feel rather euphoric. Everyone is welcoming you back and listening to your experiences with awe. You missed some things that you can now taste again. Life is good.

After a few days or weeks, you start to notice things you don't like. The waitress brings the check before you're done eating; how rude, you think. A neighbor is throwing away all kinds of things and you see this as wasteful. You prepare an ethnic salad for lunch, carefully blending fruits and vegetables for natural delicate flavor, and your guest pours ranch dressing all over it and eats with delight.

You start to feel some hostility and irritation with your culture. *How can Americans be so inconsiderate, wasteful, and mindless? Wait, I am American!* Your friends think you have gone "native" and that maybe you think you're better than they are. They're tired of hearing your complaints. Your identity comes into question and you don't know where you belong. You feel misplaced; part of you is attached to the other culture and part of you belongs here.

Over time you will adjust. I can't say things will return to normal, but you'll figure out who you are and where you belong in the moment. If you caught the "travel bug" then you'll live off the excitement from one international experience to another. It is not uncommon for study abroad students to go on three or more programs. Think of every experience as a chisel sculpting you with more details, making you more unique.

After serving in the Peace Corps, I was wrapped up in my own journey—I thought that my experiences were more significant than the experiences of my family and friends. This created a gap and some distance between us. While eventually I stopped thinking this way, I never bridged the gaps that living and working on four different continents created in my life.

Always remember your family and friends didn't experience what you did, and it's hard for them to relate to you. They had their *own* experiences and changed in ways that are different from you. New partners, marriages, divorces, births, deaths, illnesses, living arrangements, graduations, and jobs all have a major impact on people's lives. Are you focusing too much on your own experiences, and not paying attention to theirs?

Incorporating study abroad growth and development into our lives is about giving, taking, and balancing ourselves with our environment. It is about changing and staying the same. It is about seeing how big and how small we really are, all at the same time. The amazing thing about study abroad is that it affects every area of our lives and challenges us in who we are and what we do.

90. Dealing with the unexpected

I met a lot of people in Europe. I even encountered myself. — James Baldwin

One thing you can always expect is the unexpected; there will be internal and external hurdles to overcome. Don't overburden yourself with six classes and a part-time job. Take it easy and allow yourself some time to ease back into life at home and deal with the hurdles. Whether you went abroad for weeks, months, or longer, this is a critical part of assimilating your experience.

Before returning home, I applied to five graduate schools in a variety of different areas, because I knew I had to stay on track. Four of them turned me down. This shocked me after being treated with such respect in the Peace Corps. Sure, I didn't have a bachelor's degree in cultural anthropology and my grade point average was just shy of a 3.0, but I had spent four years in Africa and South America living among other cultures. Didn't that count for something?

When I returned home, it was even more frustrating when nobody would rent me an apartment. I didn't have a job, but I had enough money in the bank to pay for a full year, even more. Still, landlords wanted to see an employer on paper or a co-signer, and I didn't have either. While incomprehensible and embarrassing, I persisted and finally found someone who would accept a bank statement as proof of funds. It wasn't the best apartment in the world, but it got me through graduate school.

Change is inevitable everywhere you go so if you can learn to accept it with grace, instead of resistance; you will benefit more from it. Once your eyes are opened, it is almost impossible to close them. I still think that many things we do in the United States are stupid, but I also think other cultures I've been to can be equally stupid in different ways. Look at it as a privilege and responsibility. You are fortunate to have had such an experience, to form your opinions. Now what are you going to do about it? And how are you going to create a better world?

91. Becoming you

I soon realized that no journey carries one far unless, as it extends into the world around us, it goes an equal distance into the world within. — Lillian Smith

You know you've changed. You don't see things in the same way as before, your taste in food is different, and you hear different meaning in words. You can see a whole new world that you never knew existed. What does all this mean for you? Where will you go next? There are many decisions to make about the direction of your life. You may have some new ideas or goals or you may be confused about what you want to do.

For me, writing has always helped me sort out my life. I kept a journal throughout college and Peace Corps. When I returned to the United States, I starting writing books. My fiction debut, *Love Evil*, is the story of a young American woman who joins the Peace Corps in Africa to start over and find her way.

If you're an extroverted person, writing is probably not the way you process change within yourself. You need to be around people, talking and communicating, bouncing thoughts and ideas back and forth. The more you communicate with others, the more you will understand about your experiences and what you took from them.

Little by little, you will come to understand the value of your experience and how it has changed you. When I was in college, I took a course in cross-cultural communication. This fascinated me, opened my eyes, and changed the direction of my life. I switched my major from telecommunications to an individualized program in communication and culture. During my senior year, I was talking to some students about the Peace Corps, and I knew that was the next logical step. After Peace Corps, I had a long study-abroad career. Then my family and I moved to Italy.

One thing leads to another, but it only comes if you know how to accept and manage change. The more experiences you have, the more skilled you become at doing this.

92. Get involved

Time is a dressmaker specializing in alterations. — Faith Baldwin

It happens very often that students disappear when they come back from a study abroad experience, and we don't hear much from them again. This is truly unfortunate for us and for them. When it comes time to give out awards or recommend students, only a few come to mind.

Everyone is busy and choosing how to spend your time is an art. It's perfectly natural to ask yourself, "What's in it for me?" Getting involved with study abroad fairs, orientations, and international clubs, allows you the opportunity to network with your study abroad director and advisors, as well as international visitors, company reps, faculty, and other students. It can be a unique door-opening opportunity, especially if you are trying to break into the education abroad field.

When it comes time to interview for jobs, you will have had plenty of practice talking to people about your study abroad experience, explaining why you chose your program, what it did for you and your education, and how you are using that experience toward the development of your career. You may have acquired references from your networking activities who can support your statements.

It wasn't uncommon for my boss or the provost to ask me for student spokespersons or examples to include in brochures, reports, posters, talks, etc. I remember once an editor contacted me from *International Educator* magazine; they were doing a story on students who had carved out their own study abroad experiences instead of following the traditional path. One of our students became their shining example.

If you're looking for broad exposure, to develop your image, or brand yourself, another excellent way to get involved is through writing. Writing allows you to showcase exactly what you learned for many people. It gives you a platform that networking opportunities do not. You can write for your campus newspaper or the blog in your study abroad office, but for a national audience, submit at least one post to studyabroadmap.com (global education insights for students).

93. Credit evaluations

But there are advantages to being elected President. The day after I was elected, I had my high school grades classified Top Secret. — Ronald Regan

Be sure to have an official transcript of your study abroad coursework sent to the right office at your home institution. Allow a few weeks for it to arrive and then check to see if the appropriate person received it.

The concept of measuring credit by contact hours developed in the USA as a way to determine faculty-teaching loads. It's a costing system that isn't entirely relevant to students. In many other countries, credit is perceived as something the student achieves and cannot be measured by the number of contact hours spent in a classroom. The burden is on the student to learn, rather than on the faculty to teach.

Nonetheless, many U.S. colleges and universities still employ contact hours for determining the number of credits that will be received from study abroad. Since this formula doesn't always work—because hours spent in class are not listed on most foreign transcripts—it is common to rely on official conversion scales. For example, the *European Credit Transfer System* (ECTS) has determined that six ECTS credits convert to three or four U.S. credits. For more information, ask your study abroad advisor.

In addition to the credit conversion scales, U.S. colleges and universities account for schedule differences in their terms. This would apply when an institution that functions on three terms transfers to a system that functions on two, or vice versa. There is typically a 3:2 ratio when transferring quarter credits to semester credits and a 2:3 ratio when transferring semester credits to quarter credits. When calculating quarter credits to semester credits, divide the quarter credits by 1.5 and round to the nearest whole number for semester equivalents.

When it comes to evaluating your credit, some study abroad offices will give you credit or no-credit and some will give you letter grades that may or may not affect your GPA. Others recognize your courses as transfer credit. Grade conversion practices are not standard across universities.

A good resource that many higher institutions use to convert letter grades is the *WES Grade Conversion Guide* published by World Education Services: wes.org. If you go to their website and locate this resource, you can sign up for free access online, subject to user guidelines. You can then choose from more than 120 countries to see grade conversion scales. Not all institutions use WES.

SHAPING YOUR LIFE

94. Your stories have value

I've grown certain that the root of all fear is that we've been forced to deny who we are.
— Frances Moore Lappe

Living and working abroad shaped me into the person I am today. Nevertheless, I had a hard time articulating the values I acquired, especially to people without international experience. In these situations, I would try to find something we had in common. This would build a bridge whereby I could slip in one of my infamous stories, sure to awe.

What I've found is that people relate to stories better than they relate to experience. In fact, people love stories especially when you weave in some humor here and there. I once had a conversation with someone who asked me, "So what was Africa like?" I didn't know how to answer such a vague question, "It's not what you'd expect." Of course that didn't really explain things to my satisfaction, so I'd usually end up telling them some story.

Shortly after I started my training in Africa, I traveled north to visit a village that farmed cotton for a living. There was a gathering in the evening among the villagers, to celebrate the end of the season. The group of families had a big room, full of cotton, and I was invited to lie down in it. I stayed in the fluffy cotton for a while, until summoned to a campfire where the elders were ready to speak. There were all kinds of villagers at the meeting, from babies to seniors. It was noisy, and then suddenly quiet. It was so quiet that all we could hear were the bugs and crackling fire. A traditional elder stood up slowly, and started to speak. Her voice was coarse and deep, filled with experience.

While I didn't know who the woman was, I could sense that she was someone of great importance. All eyes were on her and everyone was silent. One of the younger men agreed to translate for me, since she spoke the native language of her tribe. She started with a few short remarks about the season and thanked everyone for their hard work in gathering the cotton. She warmly welcomed me to her village and thanked me for taking time to come. Then, she proceeded with a story about different cultures and how they can benefit from each other.

She claimed it was a true story about a young African boy from their village. Many years ago, there was an American family living in the village. They were missionaries and had young children. One of the American boys gave the African boy a stick of chewing gum. Since Africans view everything in life as being practical, the boy couldn't understand how the gum was useful, since you chew but don't swallow this substance. Bewildered, he put it away and forgot about it until one day he got sick with a bad case of diarrhea. It was so bad that he couldn't sit in class without running to the latrine every few minutes. Suddenly he remembered the chewing gum! He chewed it up and stuck it in his rear end. This helped him stay in school.

All the villagers laughed, and of course, I was baffled. I guess I was expecting some wise story about the spirit world, or something more fitting to my image of an elderly African. A joke about chewing gum as a plug for diar-

184

rhea was not on my radar, and this is what I meant by "Africa is not what you'd expect." I did learn that Africans can have an interesting sense of humor, and they can believe their humor at the same time.

95. Build on your experience

Whatever good things we build end up building us. — Jim Rohn

Building on your experience means connecting various aspects of your life. If you studied abroad in Costa Rica, and then you go to Vietnam, and then to Australia, but you can't explain why, then it looks like you're a wanderer and you don't really know what you're doing or where you belong. Believe it or not, there are a lot of young people like this, and it's okay, but when it comes time to get focused and find on a job, they have some convincing to do with prospective employers.

To get focused, consider a study abroad experience in Costa Rica, coupled with Spanish classes at home, books that you've read by *Ticas* and *Ticos*, a course on Latin American politics, membership in the Latin American club, and perhaps a few short trips to some other countries in Central America. Now this gives you a strong image and a professional edge that other students might not have. People will ask about your fascination with Costa Rican culture and you will have something to say.

Higher education is a kind of strategy. It doesn't just happen to us; we make it happen by our choices. It's important to build on your study abroad experience in the right way, on the right path. Have clear goals and work towards them. If someone asks, you should be able to explain exactly what you're doing and what you hope to get out of the experience. And whatever you hope to get out the experience should have educational or experiential value that will eventually help others.

96. Becoming wise

The only true wisdom is in knowing you know nothing.—Socrates

The word *philosophy* comes from two Greek words; *philos* means friend or lover and *sophia* means wisdom. In essence, a philosopher is a lover of wisdom, one who seeks mostly to understand. You have the dignity of a philosopher if deep down you studied abroad because you wanted to understand. It's this inner desire that drives those who are different, those who question and challenge the status quo.

Wisdom is not knowledge; it's understanding, and the first step to understand something is to realize that you haven't really understood. Nobody explained this better than Plato in *The Allegory of the Cave*, which can be found in Book VII of *The Republic*. Three prisoners have been chained deep inside a cave. All they have ever seen or experienced are the shadows cast on a wall from a fire that is burning behind them. This is their whole life and the only reality they have ever known, until one day a prisoner is released from the cave where he is astonished to see a completely different reality of people, animals, and objects casting their shadows into the cave. When he goes back to tell the prisoners the news, they do not believe it. For the shadows on the wall are the only reality they have ever known, and to them, it is all that will ever exist.

We get wisdom by going out of the cave and seeing things in a *truer* way. We see the same shadows as before, but we also see the source. This enlightenment moves us differently, taking us in new directions. There are people in our lives who won't understand our reality because they don't have the experiences that we have, and they won't leave their caves. For them, reality is their cave, and they are comfortable there. So don't blame them for this. In fact, you have to realize that you, too, are still right outside your cave. You have more to discover and a long way to go. As long as you continue this journey, you will continue becoming wise.

97. Finding the right job

If opportunity doesn't knock, build a door. — Milton Berle

If you want to get an employer's attention, you have to understand what the employer needs. There are four parts to consider: resume, cover letter, interview, and references. The goal is not be to make the employer think that you have something that you don't. The goal is to help the employer clearly see your value. If you don't weave in your study abroad experience correctly, and you don't articulate your experience in the right way, chances of getting the job are probably slim.

Your resume or curriculum vitae is a brief presentation of your education, activities, and experience. It's a summary of your value. Keep it simple and clear. With a quick glance, a prospective employer should be able to determine whether you have what it takes for the position they are trying to fill. Be sure to list your study abroad programs in the education section. If you speak any foreign languages, create a section for foreign languages and include them, too.

Every cover letter should be customized for the position and should be no longer than a page. First, go to the website of the organization and learn something about it. Make a connection between you and the organization and include this in the first paragraph.

As you start writing the middle paragraphs, highlight key action words in the job description. Then think about how you can best integrate these with your education and experience. Don't *tell* an employer you're great; *demonstrate* by highlighting, extracting, and detailing attitudes-knowledge-skills that match the job description. Part of high-quality writing is being able to pack enough valuable information into a few paragraphs, similar to packing light when you travel abroad. Your goal is not to tell the employer everything about you, but enough to get a face-to-face interview. Leave the employer curious by leaving something to tell.

Be honest in both your resume and cover letter. If you find a job that suits you well, then by all means, sell yourself as the best candidate for the position. However, if you stretch the truth or lie on your credentials, then you'll be sorry later on. Even if you get the job, chances are you don't have what they wanted and needed and you won't do well, or even worse, you'll be fired. If an employer ever discovers a lie on your resume, you can expect an immediate dismissal. This can ruin you for life.

If you are called for an interview, be prepared to talk about your experiences. While employers may believe that study abroad is a fine undertaking, it is your responsibility to articulate the relationship between your experiences and the position. Employers want to know what you learned, how your attitudes changed, the skills you acquired, and most importantly, how all of this makes you their best choice. Don't be afraid to build stories into your conversations. When interviewers asked me if I had any experience working with groups, I told them that I formed a united women's group, in Africa, from different tribes. We did small business development projects, like make soap and banana bread to sell in the market.

The interview is a chance for you to get to know them as much as it is a chance for them to get to know you. Be yourself and don't put on a show or façade. Ask questions and pay attention to the environment and office dynamics. Does it feel right? I know so many people who hate their jobs due to unhealthy and dysfunctional environments. It's important that people get along, that your supervisor is someone you can work with, and there is an atmosphere of respect. When people don't feel valued, all hell breaks loose. Remember, you'll be with these people every day!

You should have three to four references, professional and academic. It might not be a bad idea to include an international reference if it would be easy for the employer to contact him or her. Don't include more than one personal reference or relative. Don't forget to write down your relationship to each, and include at least one direct supervisor. It's annoying when people don't put the relationship on their list of references. It may be that the employer is only interested in calling one or two of your previous superiors, en lieu of your professor or friend.

When I was applying to become a director of study abroad, I was offered two positions at the same time. I liked both the positions and environments, and there was no right or wrong choice. Instead, I had to decide which one was better suited for me and my family, which was the better fit. It wasn't just a matter of salary or benefits, either. In fact, the job that I turned down was offering me 15K more than the job that I accepted. What it came down to was the office structure, the reporting lines, the people I'd be working with, the autonomy that I desired, the location relative to my parents, etc.

98. International careers

It's not your blue blood, your pedigree or your college degree. It's what you do with your life that counts. — Millard Fuller

There are options available in just about every field. When you're looking for long-term employment, pay careful attention to salary and benefits, as well as the cost of living in the job location. Make sure that your health needs can be met, and that your housing and transportation is adequate. Also, try to understand the lifestyle you will have according to the cost of living and salary you will earn.

One area that returning study abroad students often consider is international development. These workers help countries lift themselves out of poverty and raise their standard of living. While this type of work doesn't pay well, there are a wide range of opportunities: Non-Governmental Organizations (NGOs); Higher Education for Development (HED); Emergen-

189

cy, Relief, and Charity; Social Enterprise; Civil Society Groups; Private Organizations; Commercial Companies; Academic and Research; Public or Government (i.e. Peace Corps, Foreign Service, CIA); and International Organizations and Agencies (i.e. the United Nations).

You may also become an international entrepreneur. Opportunities are everywhere, and if you don't find the right ones, you can create them.

99. Graduate school abroad

Curiosity may have killed the cat, but it sure has earned a lot of people graduate degrees.
— Robyn Irving

If you studied abroad as an undergraduate, and now you are considering graduate school, there a few opportunities that I'd like to bring to your attention.

The Erasmus Mundus Joint Master Degree (EMJMD) is a prestigious, international study program, jointly delivered by an international consortium of higher education institutions. Top students receive scholarships that cover tuition fees, insurance, travel, and housing as well includes a monthly living allowance. Search "EMJMD Catalogue" for more information about programs and scholarships.

SIT Graduate Institute is known for preparing graduates as critical thinkers, good communicators, and intercultural managers of cross-cultural awareness and skills. SIT offers master's programs in Social Justice and Intercultural Relations; Teaching, Intercultural Service, Leadership, and Management; Conflict Resolution; NGO Leadership and Management; International Education; Sustainable Development; Language Teaching; Community Development; and Organizational Management.

Another program is the GlobalMBA offered by a consortium of four good universities (Fachhochschule Köln, Uniwersytet Warszawski, Dongbei University of Finance & Economics, and the University of North Florida). This unique program offers graduate students an opportunity to combine intensive classroom study with residential experiences in four different countries. See unf.edu/graduateschool/academics/programs/GlobalMBA.aspx.

The Master's International Program (MIP) through the U.S. Peace Corps offers students an opportunity to combine Peace Corps service with a master's degree program. Depending on the college or university, your assignment may consist of a thesis, project, service, or paper. MIP may also cover tuition and fees for graduate credit. Many colleges and universities participate in this program. Check the Peace Corps website for more information.

If you're looking exclusively outside of the United States, a very good book is *College Abroad* by Holly Oberle. As one reviewer put it, "Wonderfully written by a talented author with a fresh perspective. The author provides insight from first hand experiences and is not only helpful but entertaining as well. This well-written guide reads like an exciting novel. A must have for anyone thinking about getting an education overseas, traveling abroad, or just wants a great read with great advice."

100. Working in education abroad

There is a way to do it better; find it. — Thomas Edison

There are different avenues you can take in the field of education abroad. First, you have to understand the differences between the non-profit and profit sectors. Working for a study abroad company is different than working for a small study abroad office at a public university. The values are different, the focus is different, and the responsibilities are different, so pay close attention.

If you are a regional representative working for a company, then you are in sales, not education. You'll be expected to enroll students through a variety of techniques, by working with study abroad offices, going to fairs, talking about the benefits of study abroad, and lugging around catalogs and materials. Sometimes you'll be offered a trip abroad, but most of the time you'll be on the road pushing programs. Once you enter the for-profit sector, it's not easy to move to the other side of the fence.

Being a study abroad advisor or coordinator at a university means dealing with considerable paperwork and information. You may spend more time processing paperwork and taking care of problems that arise than you do talking about study abroad opportunities with students. A partner university lost someone's paperwork. Johnny is having problems getting his visa. Sally can't find a program that meets her needs. Joe needs a note taker at his host institution. Jill needs to find a counselor overseas. Professor Jim is having problems with a student who is misbehaving on a program.

This is not negative, just to prepare you for the realities of the job. I can't tell you how many times people told me that I had their dream job and they wished they were in my shoes. Surely, being a director gives you more leeway to travel, but it's still a lot of work with much responsibility. If you are in a small, understaffed office, it can be difficult to manage and you may end up spending many more hours at the office than you planned.

Study abroad professionals need a wide range of knowledge and expertise. Having been an international traveler or having just a love for international travel is not nearly enough. A good place to start is *NAFSA's Guide to Education Abroad for Advisers and Administrators*. This guide provides an overview of the areas involved in education abroad advising and administration. Written by current education abroad professionals, chapter topics range from advising students to program management to issues of financial aid to safety considerations for overseas study, as well as marketing and assessment.

Study abroad offices are often understaffed, which means that certain skill sets are valuable. I knew how to build databases in Microsoft Access and had experience as a webmaster. In every office that I've worked, these skills have proven to be valuable. So while getting more international experience or learning to speak a foreign language is important, there are also practical skills that are fundamental in the making of a good study abroad office.

Get some experience in advising by volunteering at your study abroad office or becoming a *Peer Advisor*. You can also serve on pre-departure panels or help with the study abroad fair. Study abroad advisors need a wide range of program knowledge in order to advise students properly.

Consider going back to school to get a Master's degree in international education or student affairs. You can choose another field as well, so long as it's relevant to the position you're after. Most study abroad offices are looking for people with a master's degree or higher.

Become a member of NAFSA, The Association of International Educators (nafsa.org) and attend a regional conference. There are grants available for students, sometimes covering the whole trip. You can also volunteer at the conferences to help fund your attendance.

Subscribe to the best study abroad administrator's listserv, SECUSS-L. Just search the internet since the URL is too long to be useful here.

Subscribe to facultyabroad.com and studyabroadmap.com for posts that can raise your awareness of the issues in our field. Read *The Chronicle of Higher Education* and keep abreast on what is going on in higher education around the world. A good source of information is the higher education section of the United Nations Educational, Scientific, and Cultural Organization (UNESCO) at unesco.org. UNESCO is the only body in the UN with a mandate in higher education.

Read journals, books, and research in the field: ForumEA (forumea.org), Frontiers (frontiersjournal.com), International Educator (nafsa.org), IIE Open Doors (opendoors.iienetwork.org).

Check for jobs online: Academic360.com, NAFSA's job registry (nafsa.org), Chronicle of Higher Education (chronicle.com), and HigherEdJobs.com.

It is not easy to break into the study abroad field. There's a lot of competition, but nothing is stopping you if you follow the advice in this chapter and persist in your search for the right position.

Thank you for reading this book. If you liked it, please consider leaving a review on Amazon.com or Goodreads.com.

Happy trails!

ABOUT THE AUTHER

In addition to a record of excellence, and almost 20 years of professional experience in International Education, Wendy has extensive cross-cultural knowledge and skills. Her overseas experience includes four years of duty with the U.S. Peace Corps in Cameroon and Ecuador, a two-year position in Italy, as well as short-term site visits to numerous countries around the world. She has lived and worked on four different continents and speaks English, French, Spanish, and Italian. Wendy graduated from Indiana University with a Bachelor of Arts in Communication and Culture, and from Western Michigan University with a Master's degree in Higher Education Administration. In 2014, she authored *Love Evil: An extraordinary journey of the heart* (inspired by actual international experiences and rated 5 stars by Foreword Reviews). She has also authored several articles about study abroad in The Chronicle of Higher Education.

GLOSSARY

Consortium – A group of colleges and universities that have joined forces in offering one or more programs.

Credit Evaluation – The process of evaluating a foreign transcript for credit at your home institution.

Direct Enroll – A student enrolls directly in a host institution without going through a third party.

Dual Degree – The articulation of a college degree from two or more institutions, each awarding its own.

Faculty-led Program – A travel course led by faculty members from the home institution. There may be a mix of lectures, exercises, excursions, and group time.

Globalization – The integration of economic, cultural, and political systems around the world.

Host Institution – A foreign institution from which you may take classes to count toward your degree at home.

Home Institution – The institution from which you are seeking a degree, whose requirements you must fulfill.

Integrated Program – A structured program that integrates students with the local language and culture.

Island Program – A highly structured program that clusters American or International students together within a tight framework that encourages integration with each other, rather than with the local language, community, and culture.

Joint Degree – More than one college or university's name is on the diploma, which is offered jointly and awarded by two or more different institutions.

Passport – An international identification issued by a country to a citizen that allows the person to exit and enter the home country.

Power of Attorney – A legal instrument used for the primary purpose of delegating lawful and signature authority to another.

Primary Insurance – The first policy or coverage to apply.

Resident Credit – Credit earned at the home institution or at a host institution through which you are enrolled for home institution credit. It is not *transfer credit* because the home institution accepts it as its own.

Secondary Insurance – The policy or coverage to apply after the primary insurance determination of benefits.

Third Party or Provider – A company that contracts with overseas academic institutions and housing, to *package* study abroad programs. They provide additional, logistical services to students whose other option is to direct enroll.

Transfer Credit – Credit earned at a host institution, which is accepted by the home institution toward a degree. It is not *resident credit* in the sense that it is not treated by the home institution as its own.

Visa – An official document, stamp, or seal affixed within a passport, which allows the person to enter a foreign country for a particular purpose.

CPSIA information can be obtained
at www.ICGtesting.com
Printed in the USA
LVHW041409111119
636960LV00003B/994/P